Transforming Discipleship in the Inclusive Church

Transforming Discipleship in the Inclusive Church

Stephen D. Jones

Judson Press® Valley Forge

TRANSFORMING DISCIPLESHIP IN THE INCLUSIVE CHURCH

Copyright © 1984
Judson Press, Valley Forge, PA 19482-0851

Library of Congress Cataloging in Publication Data

Jones, Stephen D.
    Transforming discipleship in the inclusive church.

    Includes bibliographical references.
    1. Christian education of adults.   2. Christian life—
Baptist authors.   I. Title.
BV1488.J66   1984   248'.5   84-14412
ISBN 0-8170-1049-1

To little Sheri.

In death, she continues
to walk in faith.

" . . . unless a grain of wheat falls into the earth and dies, it remains
alone; but if it dies, it bears much fruit."

John 12:24 (RSV)

Contents

Transforming Discipleship in the Inclusive Church

Preface

During my sabbatical term in the Philippines, I was sitting on a small wooden bench in the entrance to a school of theology on the island of Panay, talking with Rudy Acosta, a Filipino pastor-theologian. He concluded our conversation by asking, "Where is our zeal? Why is it that those of us who are open often lack the zealousness of those who are more dogmatic? Maybe openness and zealousness cannot go together. Perhaps the more open we become, the more casual we become toward the claims of our faith."

No sooner had he said those words than I felt strangely comforted that one of my struggles as a pastor was not a private concern but was a struggle felt wherever in the world the church attempts to be both "open" and "zealous."

This book addresses the question "Must inclusiveness and pluralism be sacrificed for the sake of emphasizing discipleship to Jesus Christ?" Churches that "tell" their members what to do and what to believe are more readily identified as churches demanding a "costly discipleship" (Bonhoeffer's term) than are churches that are more tolerant of diversity. Why is a tolerant church so often epitomized by casual discipleship? This book has grown out of a project in the First Baptist Church of Dayton, Ohio, which has wrestled with the meaning of discipleship in an inclusive church. The book is intended for all who love and care for a church where a crosscurrent of ideas, convictions, values, and styles of life is not only allowed but encouraged. Yet, an emphasis on diversity is not enough. The church must also call persons to discipleship to Jesus Christ. This book will endeavor to explore how discipleship can be nourished in an environment of pluralism and diversity.

The focus of the book is upon adults. This is not to say that the growth of faith and discipleship in children and youth is not important. My earlier book, *Faith Shaping*, is devoted to the development of faith in adolescents. Neither is the focus of this book upon the stages of faith development in adults. This subject has been adequately addressed in a number of recent publications. The concern here is for the nature of Christian discipleship and how that can be expressed with integrity in the inclusive church.

We are rightly suspicious of easy answers or instant solutions. We will be examining a project that was conducted within *one* church. The First Baptist Church of Dayton is still struggling with the issue of discipleship in an inclusive environment. Too much casualness toward the importance of our growth as disciples continues to exist. The motivation in sharing the findings of this project is not to give "answers," but to start a dialogue among similar churches so that we can learn from the experience of others as they learn from us. The problem will not be solved quickly. It will require that we change some fundamental expectations that we have of the inclusive church, and such change will bring pain and sacrifice.

Ever aware of the awesomeness of the problem, we can still dream of open, inclusive communities of faith that prize, at the same time, an accepting spirit, an imaginative pluralism, and an environment in which persons truly confront creative discipleship to Jesus Christ. These will be churches where persons are free to think, to grow in commitment, and to witness a variety of expressions of discipleship.

Each of the chapters of this book is designed to answer a central question of discipleship in the inclusive church:

Chapter 1: Who are disciples?
Chapter 2: What do disciples do?
Chapter 3: How do disciples grow?
Chapter 4: What is the context for discipleship growth?
Chapter 5: How do inclusive churches provide for that growth?
Chapter 6: What resources are available to inclusive churches that desire to become communities of disciples?

The project in the church in Dayton, which was also my dissertation project for the Doctor of Ministry degree, had three objectives. Let me describe them briefly.

Objective A: To provide opportunities for discipleship growth for those who sought it. The planning committee in the church provided two such opportunities: small discipleship groups and an overnight retreat. The small discipleship groups met every other week for nine months, from September to May. The groups sought to incorporate the church's diversity. They were intended to help persons grow as disciples, exercising mutual accountability in an intimate environment. The outline of the session plans for the first year of these groups is part of chapter 6 in this book. The second model, an overnight retreat, highlighted a single theme of Christian discipleship. Participants had the opportunity for individual reflection, for sharing in small groups, and for total group involvement.

Objective B: To encourage and challenge persons to participate in growth opportunities in adult discipleship. We held one training session with our boards of Christian education and deacons, who share responsibility for nurturing discipleship growth. A "learning center" approach was used, in which the board members devoted an evening to learning about and discussing the importance of discipleship groups. The pastoral staff planned worship and preaching themes that emphasized this objective throughout the year. A plan was developed for recruitment of both leaders and participants for the overnight retreat and the discipleship groups. We wanted to encourage persons who were seeking these opportunities to take advantage of one or both models.

Objective C: To redesign and have adopted by the appropriate boards the adult discipleship plan for our church that responds to discipleship growth as an active priority in the church's planning processes. Based on our learnings from this project, the planning committee wrote an adult discipleship plan that describes the small groups, the overnight retreat, and other models and approaches of our church as we provide for adult discipleship growth. The plan is described in chapter 6.

In no way was this project a venture taken on by a lone pastor in an unsuspecting church. This was a collegial undertaking from its very inception. Members of the church who were my associates in the project were Barbara Bogan (chairperson), Mike McCormick (original chairperson), Chris Twining, Vicki Arnett, Kay Berg, Don Lea, John Sheaffer, Freda Kurtz, Olivia Davis, and Mildred Schell.

Another group who gave extraordinary effort to the project were the persons who agreed to lead the small discipleship groups. The gifts of their leadership to the church and to the learnings of this project are of inestimable value. These leaders were Kay Berg, Douglas Stapp, Kevin Witt, Nancy Morgan, Gretchen Root, Ron Hawkins, Mildred Schell, Joyce Wolfe, Marian Stoner, Joe Vondruska, Marybeth Roper, and co-trainers Karen Tye and myself. In the second year, Kevin Witt and Kay Berg joined Karen Tye and me as the curriculum-writing team.

Bruce Morgan, my pastoral colleague, provided me with crucial support and encouragement during my educational pursuit.

I am grateful to James Nelson, my faculty advisor in the dissertation project at the United Theological Seminary (Dayton). Jim never told me what I wanted to hear, but always what I needed to hear. I grew to appreciate his spirit of honest, probing inquiry. These other members of the consulting faculty each made a unique contribution to the project: Donald Rogers, Roger Iddings, Emma Lou Benignus, Charles Melchert, and Tom Huguley. Typists Olivia Davis, Kathryn Williams, and Nancy Bonner have my sincere appreciation.

I owe a special thanks to Karen Tye who served as co-trainer of the small-group leaders. Karen's insight into group process and leadership is a marvelous resource to share with others.

Finally, something wonderful happened in the Jones's household in the first year of the project. Brian Christopher Jones was born on February 22, 1981, and a doctoral student became a father. The vocation of parenthood is one to which my wife, Jan, and I feel called. It is as important a calling as any other that claims our time and attention. I am particularly grateful that Brian's father is learning, in small bits and pieces, that work doesn't always come first. The little guy has not had an absentee father nor his mother an absentee husband, and yet the project was completed on schedule. How that happened I will never fully understand—the grace of God, I suppose.

Stephen D. Jones
Dayton, Ohio

Disciples, Called

Mary of Bethany is one of the most interesting disciples in the New Testament. We know Mary from three recorded incidents: a beginning conversation with Jesus at her home in Bethany, the occasion of her brother's resurrection from the dead, and the dinner celebrating that resurrection during which Mary prepared Jesus for his own death. (See Luke 10:38-42; John 11:1-46; John 12:1-8.)

Because Luke refers to Mary's family home in Bethany as "Martha's home," Martha was probably the oldest, and Lazarus, the brother, younger. It is clear that the family was widely known and respected, because of the many people who came to be with them when Lazarus died. The parents were presumably dead. In the stories about this family, Martha was definitely in charge of the household. Their village was near the Mount of Olives, on the main road into Jerusalem. Unlike many of Jesus' followers, these people were not Galileans. They may have been Jesus' closest non-Galilean friends. We can only guess how this friendship began. It is likely that the sisters met Jesus through Lazarus, who, being a male, could travel freely and extend his religious seeking beyond their village. Perhaps Lazarus was at the River Jordan with John and met Jesus there. Somehow, Jesus and Lazarus developed a friendship of mutual love (John 11:35-36).

Mary was a thinker, a seeker, and a person inclined toward courageous action as well as profound faith. These were unlikely qualities for a woman of her time. Women were not welcomed at the feet of great teachers. They were expected to do the housework. They were not to strike out in bold action but to remain behind the scenes. Mary did not fit the stereotyped roles. She was free because Martha was sacrificial in caring for the household. It is possible that Mary was so distraught when Lazarus died because, besides her natural love for her brother, he was her outlet into the world of ideas, belief, and human interaction. Being unmarried, there was no other male through whom she could extend herself.

When Jesus saw Mary weeping at the loss of her brother, "he sighed heavily and was deeply moved" (John 11:33b, NEB). He and Mary had a special friendship in which they thoroughly enjoyed and appreciated each other. Jesus had protected Mary from the household role, desiring instead to dialogue with her in the Bethany home.

The Luke text (10:38-42) offers the possibility that Martha not only questioned Mary's unwillingness to help in the kitchen, but also questioned the propriety of her sister discussing religious ideas with Jesus. Martha probably assumed that Jesus would not want to waste his time talking exclusively with a woman. As the older sister, Martha was surely accustomed to calming Mary's seeking spirit.

The discussion between Mary and Jesus was too important to be interrupted, even though Jesus risked hurting Martha's feelings. It was a conversation such as this in which Jesus extended an invitation of discipleship to Mary. From her call to discipleship came one of the New Testament's most provocative actions, the anointing of Jesus' feet with burial ointments prior to his arrest. It happened as a turning point for Jesus and his disciples. After Mary's risky act of servanthood, nothing would again be the same. Death was now on their minds.

Mary and Jesus must have had frequent conversations, for only Mary was prepared for Jesus' death; she alone helped prepare him. When all the other disciples were unprepared for Jesus' arrest and death, Mary had both a sense of the inevitable and a trust in the ultimate victory. Judas spoke not only for himself but also for the other disciples when he stated that he did not understand Mary pouring expensive burial ointment over Jesus' feet. To him, it seemed wasteful. To the others, it may have seemed morbid or inappropriate.

The passage itself only makes sense as we understand that Mary and Jesus had discussed this beforehand. Jesus probably knew she had purchased this costly ointment and was keeping it for his burial. Jesus may have said to Mary, "Mary, I appreciate your faith. You are one of the few who have faith in me beyond my death. I know that you dread my death as much as I dread it. But it is something we both know must come, for it is God's will. You have helped me accept this. And we know that the time is now not far away. ' . . . What am I to say? Father, save me from this hour. No, it was for this that I came to this hour' (John 12:27, NEB). Mary, you understand more than any of the others. You have purchased this ointment for my death. Will you anoint me with this oil when you feel the time of my death is near? Anoint me in preparation for my death and do not wait until I am dead. In this way you will prepare me bodily and spiritually for what is to come. And do this in front of my disciples, that they might also be prepared by your loving gesture.''

And so it was up to Mary to choose the time and place for her caring act. And she chose the celebration held after her brother's resurrection from the dead. In the verses just before the description of this dinner party, the Jewish leaders in Jerusalem had determined that Jesus must be killed (John 11:53). Mary knew that death stalked the door of this home, but she had learned as a child to believe in the resurrection of the dead. Indeed, she may have seen Lazarus' resurrection as a symbol of Jesus' resurrection. She alone understood.

And so it was at this dinner party for the living that she went to the place where the precious perfume for the dead had been stored. Jesus caught her movement out of the corner of his eye. Seeing the perfume in her hands, he knew and she knew that the time was drawing near. He knew that he was to be prepared for burial before his death. When Judas Iscariot criticized Mary, Jesus defended her saying, ''She has done a beautiful thing.'' The next chapter describes how Jesus followed Mary in servanthood by washing the feet of his disciples. Even then, the disciples did not understand.

The Gospels list several women named Mary at the foot of the cross and at the empty tomb. Scholars do not trace any of these women to Mary of Bethany. But one wonders how a woman who was so prepared for Jesus' death while he was alive could not also face his death upon the cross. We lose sight of Mary of Bethany after Jesus' death, but it is hard to believe that this courageous woman who so believed in the resurrection would not have been prepared for the painful events of Jesus' passion and quick to interpret the joy of his resurrection.

Mary became a disciple because Jesus invited her to be a follower. Jesus called her to this as her vocation. *Mary's discipleship began when she became self-consciously aware of being called, and it climaxed when she discovered the meaning of that calling in servanthood to Christ.*

The point at which we are self-consciously aware of being called is the beginning of discipleship. As Jesus called Mary, so does Christ invite us to be disciples. Discipleship is always initiated by a call from Christ. All the biblical evidence supports this. The call, "Follow me!" given to Simon and Andrew, James and John by the sea; Jesus' calling of Zacchaeus in the tree, "Come down, I want to enjoy fellowship at your table"; Paul's experience of being blinded on the road to Damascus—these are but a few of the many examples. Even those in the Gospels who sought out Jesus—people such as the Canaanite woman with the sick daughter, the woman with the hemorrhage, and Nicodemus—came to him because he had first reached out to others. They, too, were responding to him.

Jesus' Revolutionary Call to Discipleship

Jesus' call to discipleship was revolutionary in his day, even though the idea of discipleship was not unique with Jesus. Understanding the revolutionary nature of the call as Jesus first extended it is important to accepting its revolutionary power in our lives.

Discipleship was a common form of schooling in the first century. In the Greek world, if one wanted to learn a particular trade or become a student of medicine, one would become attached to a master or teacher in order to acquire practical and/or theoretical knowledge. In rabbinical Judaism of the first century, a disciple "belonged" to a teacher or rabbi from whom he acquired a right understanding of Scripture and achievement in religious thought. Only one who had trained under a scholar for an extensive period of time could, in turn, become a rabbi (John 7:15-16).

According to the New Testament account, Jesus was accepted as a rabbi. He was often called "Rabbi" or "Teacher" by his disciples (John 9:2) and his opponents (Mark 12:18-19). He was asked to make legal decisions just as any first-century rabbi would have been (Luke 12:13).

Yet while discipleship was commonplace in the first century, Jesus placed his own distinctive stamp upon the concept.

> Whereas in [rabbinical] circles and in [Greek] philosophical schools a man made a voluntary decision to join the "school" of his master and so become a disciple, with Jesus it was his call that was decisive (Lk. 5:1-

11; cf. Matt. 5:18ff.). Jesus seized the initiative and called men into discipleship (Mk. 1:17 par.; 2:14 par.; Lk. 9:59-62; Jn. 1:43).[1]

Thus, Jesus' call was a primary distinction of his discipleship.

Jesus' discipleship was also unique in that he did not call his disciples in order that they learn or acquire a body of knowledge. Jesus called disciples to himself. The call was not primarily for learning, but was for devotion to his own person. "A disciple's duty does not consist in maintaining and passing on particular teaching about Jesus. The essence of discipleship lies in the disciple's fulfillment of his duty to be a witness to his Lord in his entire life."[2]

A third difference with Jesus' discipleship was that one did not "graduate" from discipleship by becoming a master or teacher. Discipleship to Jesus was permanent (Luke 6:39-40; Matthew 23:8-12).

A fourth difference was that Jesus' call to discipleship had unprecedented authority. The original disciples immediately left everything behind and followed him, with no questions or reservations (Mark 1:16-20). Jesus was authoritative because his call came from God. The disciples were called to an entirely new allegiance. The old had to be left behind, as the disciples became servants of the kingdom of God on earth. Nothing else could come between Jesus and his disciples.

And finally, Jesus' call to discipleship broke through the barriers separating the sinful from the faithful.

> The very fact that Jesus calls people to follow him, and that he does this with the consequence that they leave boat and toll-office and family, denotes a quite astonishing knowledge of his mission. . . . This holds good to an even greater extent of the breaking through all barriers as in the case of Levi. Grace becomes an event in such a calling.[3]

In summary, *Jesus seized the initiative, authoritatively calling sinners to permanent discipleship to himself.* In the first century as well as in our own, Jesus Christ extends the call of God. *Christian disciples, then, are those whose lives are centered upon the call of God.*

The General and Specific Call of Discipleship

Grace is an event in anyone's calling. No one deserves to be called a disciple of Jesus Christ. While that might appear reassuring, it is not exactly good news if you are a proud person who wants to take things into your own hands, wants to be a step ahead, wants to be "in the driver's seat." And it may not be good news if you are an insecure person who does not feel worthy of being the object of Christ's attention or who feels burdened and guilty by the invitation rather than liberated. Yet this is the message of grace: Christ has already acted, already extended the invitation, already included you.

This was the message of Jesus' parable of the rich king who wanted to host a feast for his son's wedding (Matthew 22:1-14). He sent his servants out with invitations to all the important persons of the city. The servants returned stating that none of the invited guests wanted to come. The king sent the servants out again with the details of the wonderful feast he had planned. The invited guests were apathetic, rude, or even violent in their response. The king was furious. Finally, he directed his servants to go into the highways and byways and invite any who would come. Even though the invitation can be rejected, no one can attend the "wedding feast" without an invitation from the king. No one would think of attending a wedding feast unless first invited. *The invitation comes first and our response follows.* This pattern is repeated throughout our discipleship journeys.

A theology of call begins with an awareness of grace.

> For it is by his grace you are saved, through trusting him; it is not your own doing. It is God's gift, not a reward for work done. There is nothing for anyone to boast of. For we are God's handiwork, created in Christ Jesus to devote ourselves to the good deeds for which God has designed us (Ephesians 2:8-10, NEB).

Christ loves us, pronounces us worthy, and invites us to discipleship.

Discipleship not only begins with a call, but it is defined by a call. The parable of the king's wedding feast does not conclude with those from the highways being invited to the feast. One man entered without wearing a wedding garment. He came unprepared for the feast and was disrespectful of the host. He was thrown out. Jesus concludes, "For many are called, but few are chosen" (Matthew 22:14, RSV). The call to discipleship defines our response.

Christ asks that we respond to the call of discipleship with nothing less than our all. Christ wants the totality of our loyalty, trust, and gifts. As we discern this call to discipleship, we are shaped by it. Zacchaeus heard the call to give half of his possessions to the poor. The Samaritan leper heard the call to return to Jesus and give thanks. Mary of Bethany heard the call to prepare Jesus for his death. The Twelve heard the call to go out two by two, preaching and healing.

The call to discipleship can be expressed both generally and specifically. *Generally, disciples are called to embody Christ.* The call of Christ is not simply to imitate Jesus. It is not even to act as Jesus would act. The call is much more radical. Christ is to be embodied in our lives. Paul describes the nature of our call from Christ, "Your hearts and minds must be made completely new, and you must put on the new self, which is created in God's likeness and reveals itself in the true life that is upright and holy" (Ephesians 4:23-24, TEV). Paul promises, "We shall become mature people, reaching to the very height of Christ's full stature" (Ephesians 4:13, TEV). Paul confesses to the Galatians, ". . . I feel the same kind of pain for you until Christ's nature is formed in you" (Galatians 4:19, TEV).

Paul communicates this idea most clearly and frequently in his expression, "in Christ" (1 Corinthians 15:18; Romans 6:11; 8:1-2; 9:1; Colossians 2:6-7; all RSV). No affirmation expresses Paul's "in Christ" concept better than his affirmation ". . . it is no longer I who live, but Christ who lives in me . . ." (Galatians 2:20b, RSV).

> Love lives only where it is received. A person who is loved by another but does not realize it does not live "in the love" of the other. . . . He really lives in this love only when he receives and experiences the love as a participant in some sense. Love calls for love in response. Therefore Paul always understands life "in Christ" as a blessing and as a claim to sovereignty. . . . On the one hand, [life in Christ] is wholly a gift; on the other, what is given is real only when it is lived.[4]

Paul believed that life "in Christ" is a gift made real only when we both accept it and live it.

The truth is, we cannot embody Christ on our own initiative. Again, this is dependent upon Christ's initiative. "We cannot transform ourselves into his image; it is rather the form of Christ which seeks to be formed in us (Gal. 4:19), and to be manifested in us. Christ's work in us is not finished until he has perfected his own form in us."[5] Our task is to accept with openness the general call of Christ to be embodied in the lives of all his disciples.

As Christ is embodied in our lives, the call becomes specific. For Mary of Bethany, the call was to embody Christ by a sacrificial act of servanthood as she poured the burial ointment on Jesus' feet and wiped them dry with her hair. In general terms, the call to discipleship is to embody Christ throughout one's lifetime. Specifically, the nature of that call can change many times. The decision to become a father was a specific part of my call as a disciple. The decisions to minister with young people, to pastor an urban church, to be a husband, to work ecumenically—all have been specific expressions of my call to be a disciple.

We cannot expect Christ to be embodied fully in our lives on this side of the grave. That fullness is the promise of the life to come. Yet, by a lifetime of faithfulness, we will begin to approach this ideal. We embody Christ in the simplest acts as well as in the most profound experiences. We will sense our identity with Christ because of our failures as well as our victories. We will be aware of his presence as we first receive the call of Christ and then will allow this call to be expressed through our lives.

The lives of the first disciples provide helpful pictures of discipleship to Christ, though the early disciples are not necessarily the best models. Often the best models are persons in our own homes, on our block, in our church school classes, or our colleagues at work. We see these persons model the behavior of Christ in the simplicity of their beings. We see them struggle and doubt. We seem them at points of weakness and strength in their resolve to follow Christ. Our Lord has provided others to walk with us. Discipleship growth is communal as we learn from others and they learn from us. Growth happens in the context of the community of the faithful. *A community of disciples is necessary if we are to recognize the general and specific call to embody Christ in our lives.*

God graciously reaches out to us, and we are called to be disciples: ' . . . as God has called you, live up to your calling.'' (Ephesians 4:1, NEB). Nothing less than a radical commitment to growth as disciples will enable us to live up to that calling.

Discipleship and Inclusiveness

Throughout this book we will discuss discipleship and the way we grow into more faithful disciples. Often we struggle with words because they do not communicate all the desired meanings. In the New Testament, there are two primary Greek words that speak of discipleship. The verb *akoloutheo* means "to follow or accompany." It is interesting that only the verb occurs in the New Testament, stressing the action of following. The noun *mathētēs* means "learner, pupil, disciple." In both words the emphasis is upon personal growth as a dynamic quality of the one who is a disciple. A disciple is one who follows Jesus, learns from Jesus, and tries to embody Jesus Christ fully.

A disciple is not one who learns *about* a teacher named Jesus. The world of discipleship to Jesus is not a world of facts or information, but one of formation and transformation. It does not center upon the knowledge *about* Christ, but rather upon allegiance *to* Christ.

> Those who follow Christ are destined to bear his image, and to become the brethren of the firstborn Son of God. Their goal is to become "as Christ." Christ's followers always have his image before their eyes, and in its light all other images are screened from their sight. It penetrates into the depths of their being, fills them, and makes them more and more like their master. The image of Jesus Christ impresses itself in daily communion on the image of the disciple. No follower of Jesus can contemplate his image in a spirit of cold detachment. That image has the power to transform our lives and if we surrender ourselves utterly to him, we cannot help bearing his image ourselves.[6]

"Discipleship" is one of those rich, inclusive words, offered to us by Jesus himself, that express the Christian life well.

Discipleship includes inreach and outreach. It does not draw artificial boundaries between the life of the Spirit and servanthood in the world. It requires a discipline of personal devotion, as well as committed action. "Interior conversion to God is not enough if it is not accompanied by concrete effective conversion to the kingdom. . . . "[7] It includes the first-time converting decision as well as the journey of faith during which one is fully transformed into Christ's nature. It includes the tasks of evangelism and nurture. Discipleship refers not only to the individual, but also to the role of the church. It expresses the radical demands of faith as well as the universal invitation to faith that Christ offers.

Discipleship is a well-chosen word. When we speak of renewal of persons or the renewal of the church, we are on the wrong course unless our attention is focused upon the meaning and implication of discipleship to Jesus Christ. Jesus came to call persons to discipleship, and the church exists for that same reason.

Yet it is the word or language of discipleship that also presents a problem for the tolerant, pluralistic church. Like evangelism, "discipleship" is a word that has been strongly claimed by what we shall describe more fully in chapter 4 as "exclusive churches." Exclusive churches are those that emphasize conformity to one style of discipleship. They are likely to concentrate on specific content when they tell members the meaning of discipleship to Christ.

A superficial assessment may lead to the assumption that exclusive churches have the most to offer those who seek to be disciples. It is indisputable that the New Testament emphasizes the demands or costs of discipleship.

> 'If anyone comes to me and does not hate his father and mother, wife and children, brothers and sisters, even his own life, he cannot be a disciple of mine. No one who does not carry his cross and come with me can be a disciple of mine' (Luke 14:26-27, NEB).

Inclusive churches, those that emphasize their plurality, are typically cautious about making demands on their members. They tend to be tolerant, rather than rigorous, in their attitude toward discipleship. Therefore, one might assume that persons who have very clear ideas about discipleship can survive in an inclusive church but that such a church is not a good environment for discipleship growth. Because discipleship and obedience are such related terms, a further argument might be made. While inclusive churches stress the individualistic, nonconformist approach, exclusive churches call disciples to obedience by their conforming environment. We might characterize this assessment by this continuum:

The Inclusive Church	The Exclusive Church
Individualistic discipleship	Conforming discipleship

This description of the two styles clearly favors the exclusive church. Yet one wonders if such an assessment is too simplistic and superficial.

A central issue we will address in this book is whether discipleship requires conformity. Is there something to be gained by bringing together the inclusive church (where conformity is not prized) and discipleship to Christ?

There can be no argument that exclusive churches have given discipleship a definite meaning. Throughout America, "discipleship" is quickly becoming "their" word. Those in inclusive churches are apt to avoid the word as well as the concept, just as they have avoided evangelism.

Every Christian church, no matter what its style or approach, has the responsibility to employ the concept of discipleship in a way that enriches the church's purpose and calling. Discipleship must not become a coded, biased, or tagged word. It is a word for the whole church of Jesus Christ. Just as "discipleship" has become in recent years a meaningful term for exclusive churches, so can "discipleship" receive new meaning within inclusive churches. To discover this new meaning is surely the specific call of Christians and churches who seek to be faithful within diversity.

2

Discipleship in Three Words

Jesus said,

"Why do you call me, 'Lord, Lord,' and yet don't do what I tell you?
Anyone who *comes* to me and *listens* to my words and *obeys* them—I will
show you what he is like. He is like a man who, in building his house,
dug deep and laid the foundation on rock. The river flooded over and hit
that house but could not shake it, because it was well built. But anyone
who hears my words and does not obey them is like a man who built his
house without laying a foundation; when the flood hit that house it fell at
once—and what a terrible crash that was!'' (Luke 6:46-49, TEV, emphasis
added).

This passage suggests that true discipleship can be summarized in
three words—"come," "listen," and "obey."

Come

Jesus says, a true disciple is one "who *comes* to me." "*Come* with
me, and I will make you fishers of men" (Matthew 4:19, NEB). "*Follow*
me, and leave the dead to bury their dead" (Matthew 8:22, NEB).
"*Get up,* pick up your bed, and go home!" (Matthew 9:6c, TEV).
"*Go* and preach, 'The Kingdom of heaven is near!' " (Matthew 10:7,
TEV). "*Come* to me, all of you who are tired from carrying heavy
loads, and I will give you rest" (Matthew 11:28, TEV). "If anyone
wants to *come* with me, he must forget himself, carry his cross, and
follow me" (Matthew 16:24, TEV). "Let the children *come* to me . . ."
(Matthew 19:14, TEV; emphasis added in each quotation).

The vast number of words spoken by Jesus commanding pilgrimage

cannot be mere coincidence. At the core of the Christian faith is a living
Lord who says, "Come," "Follow," "Go." If this mandate were
meant only for those first disciples who could come to Jesus as he stood
beside Lake Galilee, listen to his Aramaic words, and obey, then it
would be irrelevant to us. Perhaps it was easier for them to come and
meet a person in living flesh, to respond to his words and sincerity,
and to look him in the eye. And yet Christ speaks to modern disciples
as we receive the call from the Lord of our lives: "Come unto me."

The pilgrimage of discipleship includes three complementary directions.

We are to *come together.*

It should be no surprise that we will never grow as disciples in
isolation or privacy. As we said in the previous chapter, discipleship is
not a journey to attempt alone. There are too many forks in the road,
too many obstacles, too many detours, too many risks. The Spirit, our
guide, is available wherever ". . . two or three are gathered in my
name . . ." (Matthew 18:20, RSV). But we do not simply journey
toward Christ alongside one another; rather, we journey in a fellowship
that is characterized by intimacy and accountability.

> Jesus confronts those who will listen and challenges them to *change
> radically* in a *context of support*. This is the milieu of the perceptual shift
> which is Christian growth. If either [part] of this two-pronged message is
> lost, the creative impetus of the message suffers. Challenge without support
> becomes threatening judgment; support without challenge, a secure womb
> (emphasis added).[1]

The inclusive church often fails at intimacy. Intimacy requires an
honesty that moves beyond the superficial formality that characterizes
many churches. Yet the inclusive church fails even more by a lack of
accountability. We have made our churches so voluntary, our discipleship so optional, that accountability is often viewed as an intrusion.
This is partly true because churches that do hold members accountable
are frequently those that dictate belief and piety. We therefore assume
that accountability requires a corporate mold in which freedom of
expression and growth are sacrificed.

If that were the only style of accountability available, then it would
be impossible for churches that encourage individual differences to take
discipleship seriously. But there is another style of accountability, which
we will describe in another chapter of this book. Here it is enough to

recognize that we can hold one another accountable to the journey without imposing our own way or even what we assume to be God's way.

Christ calls us to come together. This is no easy task. It requires that we enter into pain as well as joy, *with* and *for* other disciples. From the first community of disciples that surrounded Jesus, from those early resurrection communities, and throughout the history of the church, disciples of Christ have attempted to be faithful by "coming together."

We are to *come to Jesus Christ*.

This perhaps should be the most obvious part of the journey. The concept of discipleship itself is a dependent one. You cannot be a disciple to yourself. To come to Christ demands that we interact both with the Jesus of history as revealed in the Gospels and with the Christ of faith as experienced in our lives and in the world.

We are wrong to presume that Christ is experienced only by individual persons, as if a private possession. Christ is present in the world and in our lives, working in all arenas on a ministry of reconciliation and hope.

Ours is the creative task of joining Christ in this ministry. To come to Christ means to join Christ in the midst of life and ministry. For Jesus, the words "follower" and "disciple" were used interchangeably, as if the meaning were the same. Disciples are followers in the sense that we journey where Christ is already present. We do not take Christ into the marketplace. Christ is already there. We are followers. And followers are disciples in the sense that we learn at the "feet of Christ," that we might know the direction of our journey.

We are also to *come to ourselves*.

This might seem the strangest dimension of the discipleship journey, but it is important. How do we "come to ourselves"? By the very fact of our existence, have we not by definition arrived at "being ourselves"? What we seek here is to come to our most authentic selves—the selves which God created and Christ is calling us to fulfill.

> God's plan is to make known his secret to his people, this rich and glorious secret which he has for all peoples. And *the secret is that Christ is in you*, which means that you will share in the glory of God! (Colossians 1:27, TEV, emphasis added).

When I was a young boy, I loved my father's photographic darkroom.

His printing and photographic business was a one-person operation. On weekdays he was busy with customers, so photographic developing was reserved for Saturdays. Each Saturday I would go to work with my father, looking forward to being in the darkroom.

In the darkroom there were none of the customary interruptions. Once father sealed the heavy curtains that covered the doorway, no one else could enter. It was exciting to be there in the darkness and hear him unwind his negatives and place them in the enlarger. Pictures that he had taken all through the week would suddenly appear for a moment on the photographic paper below. My task was to place the exposed but undeveloped prints into the chemical solution and stir them about until the images gradually emerged on the paper. Once my father had exposed the paper and I immersed the picture in the chemicals, the picture appeared and was permanent.

Like a photographic image, the image of Christ is forever impressed into the core of our lives. No one can see it at first. It has to be developed in a faithful environment. Through a lifetime of faithfulness, this Christlikeness slowly appears as a living witness of the power of Christ's love to others.

Christ stands at the center of human life, unseen but present, ready, waiting to be embodied.

> 'Where does he stand?' He stands *pro me*. He stands in my place, where I should stand but cannot. . . . Here stands Christ, in the centre, between me and myself, between the old existence and the new.[2]

We become "incarnation people" by bringing the likeness of Christ to maturity in our lives. " . . . I live; yet not I, but Christ liveth in me. . . . "(Galatians 2:20, KJV). This likeness of Christ is more than mere human potential, though it is certainly that. It is a word whispered in the very core of our lives, which makes our existence purposeful. As the image of Christ unfolds in our lives, so unfolds our calling, our gifts, and our ministry. These spring forth as manifestations of Christ's active presence. "When anyone is joined to Christ, he is a new being; the old is gone, the new has come" (2 Corinthians 5:17, TEV). "All of us, then, reflect the glory of the Lord with uncovered faces; and that same glory . . . transforms us into his likeness in an ever greater degree of glory" (2 Corinthians 3:18, TEV).

Christ is fully, though not exhaustively, expressed in the life of Jesus of Nazareth. Christ transcends all human categories and is not restricted to being a first-century Jewish male. Christ is now expressed as female,

Latin American, Russian, black, or white. God is calling us to become what is most authentically ourselves—the fullness of our humanity, which is Christ.

When Christ says that *a true disciple is one "who comes to me . . . ," we are called to come together, to come to Jesus Christ, and to come to our most authentic selves.*

Listen

Yet the passage does not conclude here. A true disciple is one "who *comes* to me, and *listens* to my words. . . ."

To listen to Christ is no simple act; Christ speaks in ways we rarely expect. Listening to Christ requires spiritual discipline. It is surely different from hearing the words of an audible human conversation. Rather than hearing "out loud," we are more likely to be listening to Christ "in silence." Imagination is needed to hear Christ's word.

Neither the realm of faith nor the reign of God can be reached solely by rational thought. We often speak of a "leap" of faith or of "blind" faith. Faith begins where our own resources (including our intellects, wills, and emotions) leave off.

As I have observed elsewhere,

> There is today a popular misconception about the role that faith plays in human life. Many people assume that having faith means being certain and assured. They believe that faith is the solid rock, the anchor, something you can know beyond a shadow of a doubt. But . . . we don't need faith in what we "know" to be true. We need faith in what we believe or hope to be true.[3]

Rational thought attempts to grasp or take control of its object. The realm of faith cannot be grasped by thought or human will. To enter the domain of the Spirit requires a letting go, a leap of faith, a surrender. This is certainly not to say that our faith should be mindless (any more than it should be emotionless). Our intellect and our perceptions provide a corrective as we discern God's will and way. Our faith would not have depth without the ability to discern. But we take the steps of our faith journey through our imaginations. If we seek to grow as disciples, then we will need to live a life of imagination. "If the church is to be open to the presence of God in Christ now, it has to live a life of imagination."[4] We will have to train ourselves to think imaginatively. Discipleship growth is not accomplished by using a blueprint, such as a technician would follow.

Discipleship requires imagination.

We need imagination if we are to hear Christ's words, visualize the shape of the kingdom of God on earth, and discover our responsibility in it. Imagination is needed if we are to recognize the Spirit's leadership. Imagination opens the door to the realm of the Spirit. Yet, to most of us, imagination seems to be a divergence from the central task of discipleship growth. It does not appear to deserve such an important role.

> The fact that religious experience is considered so rare a thing among us
> . . . does not mean that God is no longer present, but that in our Western
> culture we have made so little of imagination, intuition, and wonder to
> discern within our own culture the presence of God.
>
> We all know how to dismiss some unlikely suggestion of an opponent.
> "He is only imagining it," we say, as if to imagine is to conjure up an
> unreal thing. We pass beyond the childlike by saying, "It is all in his
> imagination". . . . [5]

We have been taught that our imaginations are not trustworthy.

> . . . *the power of the coming kingdom of God*, announced in Jesus'
> preaching, was and *is a function of his hearers' imaginations*.
>
> If imagination were merely the fanciful, playful, childish *evasion* of
> reality which most of us have been taught that it is, then this statement
> that I have just made might border on blasphemy. If imagination were
> really the *opposite* of reality or truth, which our culture's commercialization
> and trivialization of it suggest, then my statement would be dangerous.
> But imagination is a much stouter and more central human organ than we
> have been taught. *Imagination, I maintain, is the principal human organ
> for knowing and responding to disclosure of transcendent Truth.*[6]

It is important to note the difference between imagination and the imaginary, or fantasy. Imagination is too often viewed as an escape or as an irrelevant distraction from intelligent thinking or common sense.

> By imagina*tive*, I do not mean imagin*ary*. The imaginative thought, act,
> or word puts you into history; the imaginary takes you out. The imaginative
> links the private to the public world; the imaginary is hidden in privacy.
> God's action in history can vindicate the imaginative vision; his action
> shatters the imaginary. The imaginative drives toward a transformation of
> the given; the imaginary arrests transformation.[7]

What we cannot perceive with our senses (taste, touch, hear, see, and smell), we can know with our imaginations. Imagination, therefore, can lead us to reality and open a larger world of experience to us. Most of us are unaware of how much we rely upon our imaginations. We are only aware of how much we mistrust them.

Over the past two years, my church has engaged in discipleship groups. The primary focus of these groups is to encourage the use of imagination—through prayer, through recognizing connections between personal experience and the Bible's story, through guided meditation, and through allowing the Bible to hold participants accountable for their own growth. Participants expressed awkwardness and difficulty in using their imaginations in the early part of the year together. Only after months of practice, experimentation, and risk, did they discover that new spiritual horizons were opening to them. One participant seemed to speak for others when she said,

> I fought this at first. I had no idea why you were asking us to enter the Bible imaginatively. Now I realize how important this has become to my own growth. What seemed silly at first, now seems very meaningful.

Prayer is imaginative listening. Since God is not physically present, we need a mental image of God when we pray. The image need not be a physical one, such as the grandfather on a throne with a long, white beard. Many disciples have outgrown patriarchal images, but as we pray, we must picture God in some way. I recall a number of years ago that a laywoman in my congregation interviewed me for a course she was taking at the university. She asked me, "What image or picture of God do you have in mind when you pray?" Her question utterly baffled me, and I could not understand for some time why I could not answer her question. It later came to me that one's image or picture of God need not be physical or tangible; the imagination is not restricted to picturing what we can see with our eyes and touch with our hands.

We cannot think our way to God. We cannot will our way to God. We cannot feel our way to God. We can only receive God with our imaginations, picturing and symbolizing the reality of God from our own experience, visualizing the Word of God for our lives. Imagination is our way of listening to and for Christ. It is an avenue of spiritual communication. To listen with our imaginations is to form a picture of what God through Christ is calling us to be.

When Jesus spoke of the purpose of his coming, he used one visual image throughout his ministry. He described a heavenly kingdom on earth, a coming kingdom we enter only by imagining the hope and promise that this reign of God holds for our lives and for the world.

The gospel is a gift to the imagination because in its telling of the story of the Jesus-event, in its telling the narratives of his teachings and actions, of his death and resurrection, it awakens our capacity to imagine the coming kingdom of God.[8]

. . . In friend and eventual foe alike, Jesus addressed the imagination. He addressed the eye of the heart and the emotions of the mind in such a way as to kindle the vision of God's glorious righteousness.[9]

Yet imagination should never stand alone. We must use the gift of intellectual discernment to interpret and guide the imagination. We must decide whether the images and symbols we receive/create are faithful to the kingdom, or are merely self-serving. "Ideally, reason should be richly informed by images and the development of images should be disciplined by reason. . . . "[10] "Let me underscore the point that imagination, if faithful, submits its apprehensions and constructions to the constraining and guiding norms of scripture, tradition, and reason."[11]

Christian faith is an ongoing story. Because God acted in history in the Old Testament, became embodied in the historical Christ event, and since that time has allowed the Spirit to lead the church eternal, Christian faith is a story of God interacting in time and place. We know this story both through entering it with our imaginations and through discerning it with our intellect.

Don't rush the Bible.

We want to conquer the Bible, to acquire as much as it has to offer. When we state that we want Bible study, what we too often mean is that we want to learn *about* the Bible; to know more about its personalities, message, geography, literary style, and so on. We want to rush into the Bible and glean from it as much as we can. We want to break the Bible down into manageable terms. In so doing, we often treat the Bible as a passive book of printed pages and not as the Word of life.

Knowledge about the Bible and its contents is extremely important for Christian disciples, but an intellectual approach is not the only method to be used in exploring its message. The learning that most surprised me during this past year has been the dynamic role which the Bible can play in discipleship growth.

In the discipleship group with which I was involved, we devoted nine months to a study of only four passages from the Gospels. We committed six hours, spread over three group sessions, to each passage.

We explored Jesus calling his disciples to cast their nets on the other side of the boat; the parable of the two houses, one built on sand and the other on rock; Jesus praying as his disciples slept in Gethsemane; and the ministry of Mary and Martha with Jesus in Bethany.

There were many times at the beginning of the year when I felt we lingered too long on one passage. I wanted to hurry the process. After all, there are hundreds of helpful incidents in the Gospels alone. It wasn't until the year was nearly over that I was surprised to learn that most of us want to rush through the Bible. We want to learn about the Bible, but we do not want to live with the Bible. We do not want to enter *into* the biblical message.

We do not want to give to the Bible our imaginations. Perhaps we idolize the holiness of the book or its words to the point where using our imaginations seems disrespectful. Yet without imagination, we can never enter the Bible's story so that it becomes a part of our story.

In some ways I am a changed person now because I see many more connections between my personal story and the Bible's story. I am changed because I have entered into a few biblical stories and allowed them to speak to me. I am changed because I have allowed the biblical story to hold me accountable for my growing.

When I hear Jesus calling his disciples to cast their nets on the other side, I am filled with the idea of the "new waters" in my life. When I hear the parable of the two houses, I am wondering what parts of my life are built upon shaky foundations. When I see the disciples avoiding the pain of Jesus' impending death by sleeping at Gethsemane, I wonder in what ways I am avoiding difficulty and pain. When I see Mary washing Jesus' feet, I wonder why I am not more involved in humble service.

Jesus attempted to teach his disciples to use their imaginations. He was frustrated because they did not always understand the meaning of his parables. The problem was not that the disciples were simple-minded. The problem was that they could not "imagine" Jesus' impending death and the shape of their faith in light of that. They could not "see" the reality of the kingdom of God because it did not exist in the physical world. They could not comprehend the parables because they stood outside of them. They did not enter the parables through their imaginations to discover the meanings for their lives.

When my son was a year old, he decided it was time to learn to walk. We set him on his feet, and just as they touched the floor, he would churn his way a few steps across the floor into the waiting arms of his father or mother. The motivation was not merely to walk but to be received with joy into the waiting arms of his parents. The image that entered my mind throughout this experience was of Jesus' parable of the prodigal son, the wayward child who came running home into the welcoming arms of his father. I have "lived" with this image countless times with my son, experiencing anew how our Divine Parent must feel whenever we come running into those arms of love and acceptance. I have come away with a new image of this parable's meaning. I realize that now I have played the role of the loving parent, as well as that of the wayward child. This is the way to *enter* a parable, to enter into the story of the Christian faith.

We must approach the Bible in two ways. The exegetical interpretation of the text is the more familiar and accepted path. It certainly is invaluable in discovering the meaning of the text, its language, and its historical setting. "The object of exegesis is . . . to 'lead out' of the text the meaning intended by its author."[12] The task of exegesis is important to us in preaching the Word and in remaining faithful to the Word even when we do not appreciate its message.

But exegetical interpretation must be complemented by an eisegetical approach to Scripture. *Eisegetical* means "leading in," and it can imply subjectively seeing ourselves within the Bible, its message and stories, interacting with its characters. The danger in eisegesis is that we will read anything we want to into the text; the danger in exegesis is that the scriptural account will remain detached and remote. Each approach complements the other. One represents the role of intellectual discernment and the other the role of imagination.

If we want to listen to the words of Christ, we must develop the gift to imagine as well as discern the coming kingdom into which we are called.

Obey

Jesus said that a true disciple is one "who *comes* to me, who *listens* to my words, and *obeys* them." He proceeded to tell the story of the two houses built with different foundations, as if whether or not we obey makes the final difference. The word "obey" is quite an obnoxious word to most of us. It does not have a modern feel about it. When someone barks a command at me, I find it very difficult to overcome the temptation to do the very opposite thing. But discipleship to Christ is more than simply obeying a commandment. It is not adherence to legalism. It is not taking orders. Often we wish discipleship were as simple as that.

As we come together, come to Christ, come to our most authentic selves, then we obey what we "imagine/discern" God's will to be. This is discipleship in three words: we *come* to Christ; we *listen* imaginatively and discern the meaning of his call; and we *obey* with our actions. *This triad describes the rhythm of discipleship growth.*

To obey means to take the gospel into the world. Discipleship growth can never be expressed only through an internal search. It is not only a spiritual encounter within, but is, as Elizabeth O'Connor stated in the title of her popular book, a "journey inward, journey outward."

> If we throw ourselves into ministry or social work because we cannot come to terms with ourselves, in the end we will only become a burden to ourselves and others. Persons who want to help and to do things for others or for the world without deepening their own self-understanding, freedom, and ability to love, will find they have nothing to give to others. Even with good intentions they will have nothing to give to others. Even with good intentions they will communicate only their own yearning for identity, their anxiety, aggression and ambitions, their ideological prejudices, etc. The person who wants to fill an inner emptiness through service to others will only spread this emptiness further. Why? Because every one of us has an effect on others much less through what we do than through who we are—although in our activism we often fail to recognize this fact. Only those who have found themselves can give themselves. Only those who have grasped the meaning of life can act meaningfully. Only those who have become free within from self-seeking, from preoccupation with self, and from anxiety about life, can share suffering and take it upon themselves—and free others.[13]

We obey Christ through an encounter in at least these three arenas:

We obey by an encounter with our neighbor. Discipleship leads us to an encounter with others in their need. We are called not to patronize others by sharing from our plenty, but to take on the hurt and suffering of others. Often we are even called to be vulnerable about our own hurting and suffering.

We obey by an encounter with the kingdom of God in the world. Discipleship leads us to be on the lookout for evidences of the kingdom in the world. Sometimes the kingdom is manifest by our own hard work and planning. Often it is manifest where we least expect it. Disciples work for the kingdom.

We obey by an encounter with sin. The sin we encounter may be the sin in our own lives. It may be our own failure to be all that God calls us to be. The sin we encounter may be of a personal or moral dimension. The sin we encounter may be a social sin. It may require a word or action of justice.

To obey as disciples calls us to justice when we would rather protect our own interests.

To obey calls us to work for peace when we are more concerned with our own security.

To obey calls us to give sacrificially when we would rather invest, or save, or store away.

To obey calls us to love generously when we would rather love selectively.

To obey calls us to forgive when we would rather nurse old wounds.

To obey calls us to be loyal and steadfast when we would rather act on mood or convenience.

To obey calls us to trust and enjoy when we would normally worry.

To obey calls us to risk ourselves with others when we would rather keep to ourselves.

To obey calls us to work for the kingdom of God, when we would rather work for our own selfish ends.

To obey means to embody Christ in our lives and in the world. This is the goal for all Christian disciples. And this is the result, when we come together, come to Jesus Christ, come to ourselves, and listen imaginatively and with discernment for what Christ is calling us to be and do.

3

Dying to Live

"Anyone who does not take his cross and follow in my footsteps is not worthy of me. Anyone who finds his life will lose it . . . " (Matthew 10:38-39, *The Jerusalem Bible*).

"If anyone wishes to be a follower of mine, he must leave self [centeredness] behind; day after day he must take up his cross, and come with me. . . . What will a man gain by winning the whole world, at the cost of his true self?" (Luke 9:23-25, NEB).

"Anyone who does not carry his cross and come after me cannot be my disciple" (Luke 14:27, *The Jerusalem Bible*).

As for me, the only thing I can boast about is the cross of our Lord Jesus Christ, through whom the world is crucified to me, and I to the world. It does not matter if a person is circumcised or not; what matters is for him to become an altogether new creature (Galatians 6:14-17, *The Jerusalem Bible*).

To the early church that treasured and recorded these words, the cross represented the central meaning of Christian faith. A theology of the cross emerged that had wider implications than the method of Jesus' death on Golgotha. The early church faced persecution and martyrdom. Early Christians did frequently believe unto death, as Jesus had believed unto his own death. The ultimate test of a relationship with God is that it is stronger than life or death. It is a trust that God will take care of one in death as in life. Yet the cross meant more to the early church than a willingness to give up one's life.

New Testament theology of the cross is stated in rich though obscure language. It is rooted in the words of Jesus, "No one is worthy of me who does not take up his cross. . . . " We might legitimately question if Jesus could possibly have said these words. How could Jesus have participated in a theology of the cross prior to this own death? Why would the cross mean anything to Jesus before he experienced it himself? And if he had spoken of it, how would others have known what he meant?

The authors of the Gospels state that Jesus did know of his own impending death and, therefore, could speak about the cross and its meaning. This is plausible if we do not exaggerate how long Jesus anticipated his own cross. We can be sure that some weeks before his arrest, Jesus and the disciples realized that a confrontation was un-avoidable (John 11:8-9). He had been too great a threat. His theology was too radical, his actions too unorthodox, and the political situation between the ruling Jewish parties, the Romans, and the citizenry too fragile to allow a Galilean religious uprising. Since crucifixion was the standard form of Roman capital punishment, Jesus realized that his own death by this means was inevitable.

It was at this point in his life that Jesus began to sketch the theology of the cross that would prove so memorable to the early resurrection community. This theology emerged from his earlier teachings: you cannot receive without giving; you cannot gain without letting go; you cannot succeed without taking the role of the servant; you cannot live without a willingness to die. The early church cherished these teachings of Jesus as he looked toward his own death and interpreted its meaning.

Jesus was teaching the first disciples, "The death I face upon a cross is not unlike what my disciples must face: a willingness to die in daily ways to self-centeredness, that they might be born anew into fullness of life."

> For this way of the Cross, the losing of one's life to find it, is not for Jesus alone. It is for all who will follow Jesus.[1]

> The cross is laid on every Christian. The first Christ-suffering which every man must experience is the call to abandon the attachments of this world. It is that dying of the old man which is the result of his encounter with Christ. . . . When Christ calls a man, he bids him come and die. It may be a death like that of the first disciples who had to leave home and work to follow him, or it may be a death like Luther's, who had to leave the monastery and go out into the world. But it is the same death every time—death in Jesus Christ. . . . [2]

While not as well known as other parables, a twenty-five word parable from the Gospel of John reveals the heart of what it means to grow as disciples of Jesus Christ: " . . . unless a wheat grain falls on the ground and dies, it remains only a single grain; but if it dies, it yields a rich harvest" (John 12:24, *The Jerusalem Bible*).

Here Jesus describes a pattern or paradigm for discipleship growth. Seeds do not actually die when planted, but they must be buried in the ground as if they are dead. The soil in Jesus' parable is a symbol of burial or death as well as a symbol of the nutrients that offer the possibility of life. The embryo hidden within the seed, buried beneath the ground, begins to germinate. As it breaks forth from its encasement, it grows towards wholeness.

We must likewise be willing to bury what separates us from the love of God. It must be buried and die, like a seed is buried in the ground, so that as the seed grows into full blossom, our lives might also bear a rich harvest.

This spiritual cycle of death and resurrection was first embodied by Jesus Christ in the cross and empty tomb, but it is repeated daily in the lives of all disciples. God's sacrificial action in Christ was so poignant, so meaningful, and so central to the flow of human history, that it is a paradigm for all discipleship growth. The crucifixion and resurrection of Christ form a paradigm for our maturation process as disciples. We come through to the other side, often wounded, but with a more profound sense of life's meaning than we had had before.

> Life is a series of deaths and resurrections: Disease and healing. Estrangement and reconciliation. Despair and hope. Loss and recovery. Both death and resurrection are familiar characters in our everyday existence. Death is that faceless figure with whom we wrestle all our lives, in our fear and in our darkness. And resurrection is the grasp of heaven's hand that releases death's choking grip.[3]

The cross of Christ symbolizes the dying that must occur in our daily lives. There are things to which we must die, causes for which we must die, crucifixions we must endure. There are small deaths, overwhelming losses, chosen sacrifices. We cannot experience resurrection with Christ without a willingness to walk through the valley of death.

> The first requirement of resurrection is death. We cannot choose life without choosing the death of our old selves. We prefer to ooze our way into new life, to make tiny adjustments that do not threaten who we are or how we live.[4]

Only those disciples who are willing to die to self-centeredness will gain new life. Only in dying will we gain a glimpse of the new life toward which Christ is calling.

This message comes to us in a rare example of Paul using a parable of Jesus to make a similar point:

> When you plant a seed in the ground, it does not sprout to life unless it dies. And what you plant is a bare seed, perhaps a grain of wheat or some other grain, not the full-bodied plant that will later grow up (1 Corinthians 15:36-37, TEV).

It was Paul's task to develop further a theology of the cross, and he does this in his letter to the Romans,

> By baptism we were buried with him, and lay dead, in order that, as Christ was raised from the dead . . . so also we might set our feet upon the new path of life.
> For if we have become incorporate with him in a death like his, we shall also be one with him in a resurrection like his. We know that the man we once were has been crucified with Christ, for the destructions of the sinful self. . . . If we thus died with Christ, we believe that we shall also come to life with him (Romans 6:4-8, NEB).

Because of the resurrection of Christ, we know that resurrection always stands on the far side of crucifixion and death. This is where the resurrected Lord stands in our lives.

> 'Where does [Christ] stand?' He stands [for me]. He stands in my place, where I should stand but cannot. . . . Here Christ stands, in the centre, between me and myself, between the old existence and the new.[5]

Christ stands between the cross we are to carry and the new life to which we are called. Christ stands between the voice of compromise, self-pity, or fear, and the voice of hope.

The cross we are to carry is not a punishment that must be endured before good times can be enjoyed. We are not left alone, confused, and divided. Christ stands in the midst of our deaths and resurrections. Christ stands where we cannot stand alone, guiding us through the spiritual paradigm for growth. Without the advocacy and presence of Christ, there is no basis to believe that hope arises from the ashes of loss and despair.

Jesus said that his disciple will "take up his cross daily and follow me" (Luke 9:23, RSV). It is not something that happens once or twice in the life of a disciple. It happens daily. In the third chapter of the Gospel of John, Jesus used another image to teach this to a leading Pharisee by the name of Nicodemus. Jesus told Nicodemus that he had to be born again if he was to experience the kingdom of God. Some strictly interpret this to mean that there are only two births: the first birth into life, and the second into new life in Christ. Yet other translators see more variety in the text. The Greek word in the text can also be translated as "born anew" or "born from above." To be "born from above" is to be born into a kingdom not "of this world" and carries the connotation that it can happen over and over again in the disciple's life. As Paul said, what matters is for a disciple "to become an altogether new creature" (Galatians 6:15b, *The Jerusalem Bible).* This only happens as we carry our cross in daily ways. To become disciples of Jesus Christ is not merely a one-time decision but a lifelong pilgrimage in which we each become "an altogether new creature" in Christ.

This is not to degrade the importance of first-time decisions to follow Christ, which all disciples make, implicitly or explicitly. But if our understanding of discipleship is consumed by a "saved-lost" mentality that values only first-time decisions, then we are doomed to a superficial and, therefore, unfaithful discipleship.

> When we are born from above we accept the meaning and reality that are constructed by God rather than by ourselves. We step out of the planetarium of human purpose and look into the real sky of God's universe. The stars that guide us are no longer the values which we project, but the truth which God makes to shine.[6]

Through discipleship groups in our church, we learned what a difficult thing it is to interpret our own growth through the death-and-resurrection paradigm. For many of us, the words "death" and "resurrection" are used too exclusively in reference to events in Jesus' life to have any meaning in our own. Of course it is not the words themselves that are important. But any model for discipleship growth that does not call us to die so that we might live is not heeding the teaching which Jesus offered. The call of disciples is to so embody Christ that we embody his death and resurrection.

We need to relate the call to die that we might live to our human experience. The call to die to self-centeredness can be heard in at least these ways.

The dying to self-centeredness can be a giving up:
    giving up bad habits,
    giving up negative attitudes toward ourselves or others,
    giving up fear of the unknown.

The dying to self-centeredness can be a <u>letting go:</u>
   letting go of one set of priorities for another,
   letting go of that which is trivial or superficial,
   letting go of a craving for security in order that we might learn to
      trust more,
   letting go of false idols to which we cling.

The dying to self-centeredness can be a <u>willingness to sacrifice:</u>
   willingness to sacrifice what we desire so that others can have
      what they need,
   willingness to sacrifice the security of a job or career to which we
      no longer feel called in order to enter a new arena of work or
      service,
   willingness to sacrifice as a volunteer for others.

The dying to self-centeredness can be a <u>willingness to suffer:</u>
   willingness to view physical suffering as a vehicle for communion
      with God,
   willingness to suffer for our beliefs,
   willingness to pay the price for speaking out for justice and lib-
      eration,
   willingness to suffer from ridicule or misunderstanding.

The dying to self-centeredness can be a <u>willingness to give our own</u>
<u>lives in death</u>, if necessary, should God call us to do this.

The death may be within us—the death of false idols, false dreams, selfish ambitions, destructive habits, and harsh judgments. Paul promises, "For since we have become one with him in dying . . . we shall be one with him by being raised to life . . ." (Romans 6:5, TEV). Jesus invites us to leave the security of our tombs, to abandon the burial clothes, and to step forth in the light of resurrection. "O death, where is thy victory? O death, where is thy sting?" (1 Corinthians 15:55, RSV). From the death we endure and the cross we carry, Christ offers the promise of new life. We have but to knock, and the door will be opened to us.

I recall vividly when Lillian reached out for my hand, her black hand in the palm of my white hand. Friend to friend, we gazed with respect toward each other, knowing the painful reality of her situation. After prayer together at her hospital bed, Lillian said with certainty, "I do have faith. God will use my suffering for some purpose." She lay there before me, nearly unrecognizable. Her face was bloated from radiation, her head bald, her body paralyzed from the waist down. Her husband was unexpectedly out of work. And she was talking about faith, about God using her suffering, using her cancer.

I knew in that moment how sorry I was to admit it, but I do not have faith like that. It may have been because of my younger age or untested experience, but as I stood there looking at this woman of profound faith, who understood mystery, subtlety, and pain, I could not understand her willingness to follow God into whatever death gripped her.

I thought to myself that I would be mad as hell to have lived her life, to have suffered in the ways she suffered, and then to have to face such a slow, agonizing death. I would be filled with relentless anger.

The death to which Christ calls us, whether it be our final death or the daily task of carrying our cross by dying to self-centeredness, is never without pain or cost. We rarely enter it without hesitation. Yet to live, the grain must first die. This is the call of those who would be disciples.

4

The Including Community

"The Includer" aptly describes Jesus. His was a ministry of including persons previously excluded: tax collectors like Matthew and Zacchaeus, adulterers who had been sentenced to death, lepers who had been condemned to isolation, Samaritans like the woman at the well, women like Mary of Bethany whom Jesus elevated to the unlikely role of his student, pagans like the Canaanite woman whose daughter was healed, criminals like the one who repented from the cross, and children whom Jesus called to his side rather than relegate to roles of lesser importance.

Jesus' ministry also included those who were alienated from one another. "Should I forgive my brother seven times?" Jesus was asked. And he responded, "Seventy times seven" (see Matthew 18:21-22). He included the lost and the forgotten in his parables about a lost sheep and a lost coin. Indeed, a central purpose for Jesus' life was to include all of humanity in God's activity of salvation, to include this world and this life as well as the life and the world to come in the kingdom of God.

This characteristic of Jesus is the reason why the community that calls itself Christian needs to be an *including* community. Churches, by their style of worship and ministry, may appeal to a certain segment of the population, but the purpose of every church remains to include all persons, no matter their condition or situation. The divorced, the handicapped, the famous, the unknown, the powerful, the impotent, the clean, the smelly, the alcoholic, the suicidal, the opinionated—all are in need of the church's healing ministry and of Christ's redeeming presence.

Styles of Churches

The way in which churches respond to the diversity of their members is the object of our attention here. I am a pastor of what I call "an inclusive church." Inclusive churches are not necessarily better, but it is my conviction that inclusive churches do have something unique to bring to a renewed emphasis upon discipleship, and something unique to gain from such an emphasis.

An *inclusive church* is a local congregation that recognizes, respects, highlights, and celebrates the diversity of its members. It is a church that encourages a diversity of theological belief, and protects the expression and forum of faith from censure or condemnation. It is founded upon the historic principle of "soul liberty" (a free-church term for the freedom to interpret faith in the light of individual conscience). It is likely to have a "free" pulpit, in which a pastor is given freedom to proclaim whatever he or she feels led by God to preach. It is likely to be ecumenical and to have an open, accepting environment in which tolerance or respect (terms to be defined later in this chapter) are prominent. Often persons in an inclusive church come from a variety of life-styles, neighborhoods, and economic levels, as well as theological commitments. Unfortunately, in its eagerness to be open, the inclusive church frequently has lukewarm expectations of its members and fails to lay sufficient emphasis upon the radical obedience of discipleship to Jesus Christ.

A *homogenous church* is a local congregation that minimizes the diversity of the members and highlights consensus. It is a church that promotes uniform expression of theological belief, though it will not likely censure other expressions as long as they are not qualitatively different nor powerfully articulated. Some homogenous churches prize one style of faith but are accepting of others. These churches may be ecumenical in spirit. Others are not so accepting and will minister comfortably only with similar churches. The predominant faith style or theological belief of the homogenous church is often taken for granted by its members. New members are expected to be assimilated into the church's mainstream of belief and practice.

An *exclusive church* is a local congregation that minimizes the diversity of the members and highlights uniformity of belief and practice.

It is a church that tolerates only one expression of theological belief. It will often not accept other approaches to faith. The exclusive church tends not to become involved in cooperative efforts with churches that are different from itself, though it might cooperate with like-minded groups. The exclusive church will tend to be highly vocal about Christian discipleship. It will define discipleship in a quite specific fashion and train its members in accordance with that definition. Prospective members are expected to accept this approach (if they cannot, they are not included). In the exclusive church, there is some internal order of discipline that monitors divergent belief, though this may be so subtle or informal as to be unrecognized by its members.

The *cultural church* is a religious group in which a whole culture is in the church by virtue of birth or nationality. The European state church or the model of the Roman Catholic church in many Latin American countries are examples. In the United States the churches of ethnic groups with strong ties to Europe or Latin America can often be identified as cultural churches. The only way to escape belonging to a cultural church in such a society is to renounce it. Often persons participate nominally in religious celebrations as cultural events but have no personal discipline in belief or practice of faith.

Comparing Inclusive and Exclusive Churches

This book is written for the inclusive church, yet it is not to be viewed as an attack on the exclusive church. Many people find themselves vulnerable in the midst of pluralism. The crosscurrents of an inclusive church leave them tossing and turning without a solid anchor. They need the external discipline found in the exclusive church. In the best sense of the word, they need to be told what discipleship to Christ means and how to live it. Yet, others find themselves smothered in a community that demands conformity to one belief. An exclusive environment stifles their freedom to choose. They need the stimulation of personal exploration and the cross-fertilization of ideas among fellow seekers.

Both inclusive and exclusive styles are needed; each can play a helpful role. The historic patterns of those converted in exclusive churches migrating to inclusive churches to continue their growth, and of those reared in inclusive churches migrating to exclusive churches to discover the fundamentals of faith, bear witness to the complementary roles of the two styles.

Exclusive churches tend to offer a specific statement of belief or practice, and this is more easily interpreted to those outside the church. They can say, "This is the one true answer. This is what we believe. This is how we act." There is little ambiguity in their message. Inclusive churches have the more difficult challenge. They say, "We are disciples of Jesus Christ seeking to understand what this means for ourselves and our world." While exclusive churches are often better in stimulating the first-time conversion, inclusive churches are more apt to enrich the task of lifelong transformation to Christ. If, indeed, one natural advantage of the inclusive churches is transformational growth, then these churches must discover ways to emphasize discipleship so as to enable this growth.

The emphasis in the inclusive community is on whom it includes. In a strong inclusive community the focus is upon respect for differences, the shaping of a definite environment that defines for the community broad parameters of belief and practice, and a "pilgrimage of growth" in which persons are uniquely transformed into the image of Christ.

The emphasis in the exclusive community is on a single affirmation of faith. Those who cannot affirm the definition of faith and practice that is at the heart of the community are excluded. A strong exclusive community easily articulates what unites its members.

It is important to treat with care the definition of the inclusive and exclusive church. If pushed to an extreme, every church includes some persons, and thus no church is completely exclusive. On the other hand, every church excludes some persons, and thus, no church is completely inclusive. The definition of "inclusive" or "exclusive" is directed to the emphasis of a church. *The emphasis of an inclusive church is upon plurality, and the emphasis of an exclusive church is upon conformity.* How diversity is handled is what characterizes an inclusive or exclusive church. It could be that a church with a wealth of pluralism is exclusive because it emphasizes conformity in the midst of its pluralism. And it is possible for a relatively homogenous group to be an inclusive church because it emphasizes and celebrates the diversity that does exist.

Inclusive churches need not attempt to be all things to all people. They need not vary their form of worship, their structure of decision making, their very life together, to attract every type of person in society. But in their life together as people of God, they must find ways to affirm their plurality and use their inclusiveness as a resource for faith rather than an obstacle to faith.

Neither can we attach automatically the labels "liberal" and "conservative" to inclusive and exclusive churches. There is perhaps a tendency of inclusive churches to be more liberal and of exclusive churches to be more conservative, but the stereotypes are not universal and are distorting.

Some liberal churches are far from inclusive churches. Indeed, the more singularly liberal (or conservative) a church is, the less inclusive it tends to be. Consider for example some suburban churches where the pews are filled with middle-aged, middle-income families who desire nothing but to fill more pews with "their kind of people." This describes an exclusive church. It is possible to be liberal and exclusive. This kind of exclusivity dictates (probably subtly) a liberal dogma or creed upon the members and disdains more conservative approaches. It is also possible, though perhaps less likely, for a conservative church to be an inclusive church. The emphasis of such a church might be on the fundamentals of faith, while it encourages variety in the ways these fundamentals are explored and expressed. Obviously, homogenous churches can be of any theological opinion.

The difference between the inclusive and exclusive church may be most obvious in these distinctions:

1. *The way in which the church highlights or ignores the diversity that exists within its own membership.* If people are encouraged to express themselves and grow in directions that may be unique from the majority of the church's leadership, then such a church is inclusive. If decisions of faith or discipleship tend to follow a hierarchical model, from the center of the church's leadership outward, or from the top down, then such a church is exclusive.

2. *The way in which the church approaches new members.* Homogenous evangelism, in vogue today because of the church-growth movement, is an attempt by a church to seek like-minded people or those who will conform to the existing membership of the church. This style of evangelism is typical of the exclusive church. It offers security and certainty to those who need it. Inclusive evangelism, the kind of evangelism that is typical of the inclusive church, also seeks a particular kind of person. It seeks persons who enjoy diversity and who can grow toward Christ in the midst of it. Inclusive evangelism offers challenge and freedom to those who need it.

One problem that has faced evangelism in the inclusive church is the tendency to privatize faith, which is the result of an emphasis upon individual expression. Churches that effectively foster evangelism are usually those in which persons freely and frequently talk about faith with one another. They are then able to take the invitation to discipleship beyond the fellowship of the church. As persons in inclusive churches learn to share their faith within community, they can become effective evangelists.

3. *The approach to learning within the church.* Inclusive churches will be typified by dialogue. Learning in these churches will be a give and take, and there will be a dissatisfaction with any position as "final" or complete. In dialogical learning, persons share with one another in the expectation of being engaged in conversation and of being transformed by it. Learning in the exclusive church is typified by monologue, a monologue not in the sense that only one person is talking, but in the sense that only one point of view is being expressed by everyone. The exclusive church's approach to discipleship will be clearly defined, and the educational search will be to find ways to speak it with greater clarity and appeal. Socialization or acculturation occurs in any human community. The socialization in an inclusive church encourages freedom of response, whereas in the exclusive church it encourages conformity of response.

Limits of Inclusive Churches

There must, of course, be limits on inclusive churches. They need to have a certain kind of "glue" that holds them together, and tolerance of individual differences is not enough. It is important for an inclusive church to stand for something. If pushed and pulled in too many directions, fragmentation and disharmony result.

Leonard Sweet has written an insightful article on the fear of some churches to affirm any certainties or answers or truths.

> Certainty holds too many terrors for liberalism, and uncertainty too few.
> . . . Liberalism has exhibited a lazy satisfaction with proclaiming cross-eyed paradoxes and crossroads ambiguities, large questions and tiny truths, as if this is the best we can hope for. . . .
> Life without a centered faith suffers extreme spiritual discomfort. The idea that God has not given us some answers to our questions is intolerable to the human spirit, driving us to the very edge of fatalism on one hand, or fanaticism on the other. . . .
> The world does not want to know Christians' speculations; it wants to know our affirmations and certainties. . . .
> When affirmations are negations, declarations are doubts, and answers

are questions, "truth" is dressed in ill-fitting clothes that are inadequate to protect people from the cold and rain.[1]

Even though liberal churches are not necessarily the same as inclusive churches, Sweet offers an accurate critique of the inclusive church. In wanting to stand only for pluralism, many inclusive churches are fearful of standing upon any truth or certainty. Yet pluralism alone is not an adequate grounding upon which to stand. If a church is to be truly Christian, then the fabric of the gospel must be integral to the life of the inclusive church. If a church attempts to represent anything or everything, then it will not be a church for Jesus Christ.

The inclusive church operates within a framework, seeking members who find that framework helpful. It invites misery when it welcomes participants who cannot share the framework of faith upon which the inclusive church is based.

Commitment to Christian discipleship can be the "glue" for an inclusive church. The boundary for an inclusive church that follows this commitment is that all growth must be "toward Christ" or it is unacceptable. Actions must be perceived to be Christlike, or they are unacceptable. Inclusive churches recognize that Christ is received in unique ways, and, by their very nature, will not restrict these interpretations. But, if inclusive churches are serious about discipleship, the test of their common actions, personal discoveries, and aspirations will be: Does this move us toward Christ? Is this Christlike?

Each inclusive community, under the authority of the Bible and the power of the Holy Spirit, will need to marshall its imagination and wisdom to answer these discipleship questions. In the asking and answering of these discipleship questions, inclusive churches can discover their faith identities.

Four Primary Words of Renewal

Concern for discipleship in the church is a concern for renewal. This concern is not primarily for institutional renewal, though certainly that is affected. The renewal that is sought is, rather, a renewal in the church by the Spirit, and of persons in the Spirit. It is a renewal of the mission of the church, both through inreach and outreach. Discipleship is a rich concept that not only encompasses both of these but also pulls together into a theological whole both directions of the Christian journey. Discipleship cannot be an inner spiritual renewal at the expense of servanthood in the world; yet, neither can it be an active outreach that neglects renewal of the inner life.

I want to suggest four primary words for the renewal of the inclusive church. Much of what follows could also apply to exclusive, homogenous, and cultural churches. Our focus, however, is on the inclusive church and its possibilities for renewal.

The First Word: Commitment to Discipleship

Many churches spend far too much time congregating and far too little time "discipling." They presume that the more time members spend together, the stronger the church becomes. In fact, the direct opposite may be closer to the truth. It may be that the more time spent in the world in personal or social witness to Christ, the stronger the church becomes. It is the world for whom Christ died, and we diminish our effectiveness as persons who represent Christ by committing the largest portion of our available time within the church away from the problems and needs of the world. If this assumption is true, then the time spent together is precious and needs to be focused upon preparing us for ministry and upon giving tangible meaning to discipleship. In and of themselves, there is nothing wrong with church bazaars, socials, craft groups, athletic teams, and so on. In fact, these can serve important purposes. But too often we become so busy congregating that we diminish the time we have for discipleship.

Inclusive churches do not tend to monopolize the time of their members by planning congregational events for every spare moment in the week. Potentially, there is more opportunity for members to express their discipleship in the world. The church community is challenged to focus time upon the theological meaning of discipleship. Together, the congregation members can recognize and verbalize the ministries to which they are called. Together, they can support and train one another. Yet, even in the precious time that members of inclusive churches spend together, "congregating" events often consume too much attention.

As indicated in chapter 2, the goals of a commitment to discipleship are to come together, to come to Jesus Christ, to come to our most authentic selves, and to listen imaginatively and with discernment for how Christ is calling us to act and to obey. The renewal of the inclusive church begins with this commitment. Discipleship is not concluded with one decision of life, nor it is a "caught" by our merely congregating with other Christians. The call from Christ to be disciples is radical, and nothing short of a total commitment will enable this call to be actualized in our lives. The logic of the gospel is not common sense; in fact it runs contrary to common sense. Thomas Troeger has rightly described the inverted logic of discipleship:

> We are like the bottom bulb of an hourglass. All our lives people have been funneling care and strength into us. From our mother's milk to the books in the public library we have depended on someone else's presence and knowledge. . . .
>
> The greatest threat in the world is to turn the hourglass upside down, to reverse the flow, to pour ourselves out. . . .
>
> Salvation means to be turned upside down so that all the love and nurture that God has poured into us now pours out of us into the world. Jesus Christ inverts us through his teaching, through his relationship to us, and through the way he reconstructs reality.[2]

One member of a small discipleship group in our church stated in the last session of the year that she had felt satisfied for many years with a simple faith in which she called upon God to solve the difficulties or challenges she faced. Now she felt God was calling her to join in the struggle by facing some of the challenges and living more with the questions. She said she now felt like a young child learning to ride a bike when, for the first time, the training wheels had been removed. Her comment was interesting because I had just shared with the same group that I felt my calling was to diminish my need to control things or to keep my finger on all situations. I was learning to let go and trust God working through the process and through other people. Headed in the opposite direction from my friend, I, too, felt as if I was learning to ride a bike without the security of the training wheels. A commitment to discipleship in the inclusive church is not a search for the one true model toward which we should grow in united syncopation. We will often find ourselves called in diverse directions; yet we will learn from this diversity. This woman has much to teach me about trusting God. I have much to offer her in facing the challenges.

Discipleship in the inclusive church will require an approach in which each person can be taken seriously because the call of God is not standardized. The inclusive church will need to deal with each disciple as an individual with a distinct call from God and special ministry to perform. Christ may be experienced in as many ways as there was disciples.

We have found diversity to be our richest resource for discipleship growth. The variety has been instructive. The inclusive faith environment is a great respecter of persons and, indeed, has the capacity to call forth the best from them. We have not felt threatened in coming together because we have not felt as though we were being spoon-fed or having something forced upon us by others. The call and meaning of discipleship has emerged from within the interaction of a seeking group of Christians. In the inclusive community of disciples, we cannot be judgmental, for we recognize that the inverted logic of our Lord is a knowledge that ". . . can never be fully known . . ." (Ephesians 3:19b).

The Second Word: Accountability

The roles that accountability plays in inclusive and exclusive churches are different. In the exclusive church, accountability is enforced by the community. The freedom of choice of the individual is limited to deciding whether or not one wants to be a part of such a church. Once that is decided, the community determines which directions of spiritual growth are valued and which are not. Persons are not necessarily exploited, but individual freedom is sacrificed for conformity to community expectations.

In the inclusive church, each person must make the final decisions as to how he or she wants to be held accountable by the community and what constitutes his or her most authentic self. Others will influence that decision, but in the end, the decision belongs to each person who undertakes a journey of discipleship. Persons will participate in accountable groups only through their own choices. They will be held accountable, and they will hold others accountable. There is no sense in which growth or accountability is forced upon anyone. The result of accountability in this context is that each one experiences freedom to grow in the direction he or she believes Christ is leading.

It would be an error to assume that the accountability structure of the inclusive church is individualistic and that of the exclusive church communal. Accountability is always interpersonal and, therefore, communal. It occurs between persons and between persons of God. The difference is that in inclusive churches the freedom of persons is paramount; while in exclusive churches the will of the community is supreme.

Accountability is easier to introduce into an exclusive church because it ensures that its members don't become like other people. Accountability in an exclusive church is an important "group protection policy" that serves an institutional function: it tempers differences and accents commonalities. While accountability serves no such survival role in the inclusive church, discipleship growth can never be taken seriously if the church ignores the issue of accountability.

Accountability need not be harsh judgment nor a sign of mistrust. Rather, it can be a sign of loving concern. If a faith community has no expectations of its members and, therefore, no mutual accountability, it is limp and apathetic. Accountability is neither rude nor unnecessarily blunt. It is not unkind. On the contrary, it is to be so kind as to speak the truth lovingly: ". . . Let us speak the truth in love; so shall we fully grow up into Christ'' (Ephesians 4:15, NEB). An accountable relationship is one that focuses our lives upon the mutual commitments we have freely made. It places no value upon the superficial or the artificial. We demonstrate a lack of love when we retreat from the truth in fear of holding another to the path he or she has chosen.

God is love, but God holds human beings accountable. God's accountability does not force or require us to do anything, but there are consequences to our actions and to our commitments. The theme of judgment is the New Testament's primary way of dealing with the issue of accountability. I recall the love that motivated Jesus to awaken his disciples three times in the garden of Gethsemane so that they might watch with him. It was typical of the way in which he expected the best from them and held them accountable. We rarely interpret the disciples speaking up at the home in Bethany (when Mary poured expensive ointment on Jesus' feet) as a demonstration of accountability, but it can be interpreted that way (Matthew 26:8). Jesus and his disciples openly practiced a mutual accountability that held them to their courageous course.

When Jesus speaks of judgment, he does not describe a harsh, vindictive God anxious to get even with us for our sins. Rather, he describes a God who is loving enough to expect our faithful response; he describes a God who cares enough to discipline us with the consequences of our unfaithfulness. The primary message of the gospel is never "God punishes." It is, rather, "God cares and God forgives." Confession and forgiveness are the practices of accountability.

The truth is that we lack both the insight and the inclination to keep our lives on course unless we have accountable relationships with other people. We tend to round off the demanding edges of discipleship when we are free to rationalize and compromise by ourselves. Christ works through accountable relationships to call us to faithfulness. Friends in the faith who love us enough to hold us accountable to our professed commitments are dear friends, indeed.

Nevertheless, accountability is one area in which inclusive churches too often fail. The more that exclusive churches hold their members accountable to a prescribed course, the further inclusive churches stray from holding any expectations of one another within their congregations. Inclusive churches often presume that being accepting of others means that accountability is an intrusion into another person's private domain. They have an unwritten agreement: "You deal with your faith; I'll deal with mine. We won't get in each other's way."

Inclusive churches pay dearly for their reluctance to engage in mutual accountability. Several years ago I called on new members to our church, and the couple shocked me by stating that they had joined our church because we have few demands or expectations. They felt that we have a more "laid-back" approach, which they appreciated. I pray that they are wrong in their perceptions, for I have a difficult time finding a scriptural basis for a church that makes few demands and is so casual about faith that it attracts the spiritually lazy. Yet I recognize that this is a common struggle for inclusive churches that have found it difficult to incorporate accountability into their corporate life.

For me, "holding one another accountable" conjures up an endearing image of being held lovingly by another. Accountability need neither be hierarchical or stereotyped; it never need sacrifice inclusiveness. The opposite of accountable love is careless love: "I love you, but not enough to intercede on your behalf"; "I love you, but not enough to hold on to you accountably."

We are frightened of accountability because it demands honesty and vulnerability. It demands that we take one another seriously. It demands knowing when to speak and when to be silent. It demands posing questions that help one another to clarify meanings and callings. It demands that we help focus one another's faith. Without accountability, we are left with a lukewarm faith that possesses no life force and no converting power.

A central question of our quest to grow as disciples through our church has been "Can we hold one another accountable within a variety of expressions of discipleship, without dictating one form of expression?" We have discovered that we can be mutually accountable to one another in our diversity.

The Third Word: Respect

Inclusive churches tend to be centers of tolerance. Only recently have I understood what a weak commitment tolerance can be. It certainly is no substitute for respect. Tolerance is passive. If I tolerate you, I am not required to take any action toward you. I just allow you to "be." In effect, tolerance only requires putting up with another person. It does not demand anything other than a passing knowledge of another person. Tolerance does not require that we agree. It does not require that we "come together."

On the other hand, respect is active. If I respect you, I am required to reach out to undergird and support you. Respect surrounds another person with appreciation for who he or she is. It does not require that I agree with or imitate that person. I cannot remain detached from those whom I respect. I pull those persons into my circle of concern.

The problem with tolerance is that it allows us to remain indifferent toward one another. Respect demands that we support one another, that we take the first step of discipleship and "come together."

One of the strongest statements an inclusive church can make is in the covenant of the First Baptist Church of Dayton, which was written by the congregation in 1978. It states that we covenant "to respect the diversity of belief among ourselves as together we mature in Christian faith."

Moving from tolerance to respect in the inclusive church is a subtle change, but the result is significant. When we respect one another in mutual accountability, we never have to fear that the inclusiveness of our church will be compromised.

The Fourth Word: Intimacy

This word is implicit in the first three words. The inclusive church cannot take seriously a call to discipleship that is not implemented in structures small enough to take individual persons seriously. Both accountability and respect demand intimacy. Strangely, that which we most desire, we also most fear. Intimacy is what we prize most highly, and yet our fear of it is great. As disciples, we come together intimately, come to an intimate knowledge of Christ, and intimately come to know the self that God is calling us to be.

Inclusive churches find it all too easy to encourage privacy and all too difficult to achieve intimate relationships. The person who seeks to remain anonymous can do so easily in a setting that is so eager to avoid invasion of privacy that it all but ignores the individual. It is often believed that the duty of the inclusive church is to allow members to remain side by side in the same pews but never to enter one another's lives. This makes a mockery of the "oneness in Christ." Jesus promised to be present wherever "two or three are gathered in my name." To be gathered in the name of Christ does not mean merely to be physically in the same place, but rather to be intimately joined to one another through Jesus Christ, who unites us. The presence of Christ is greater when we gather in intimacy.

One participant in our small discipleship groups stated that his major learning was that as he came to know others intimately, he realized that their struggles and concerns were similar to his. This revelation can help lay to rest a fear that many of us have. We assume that other people are made of different "stuff." We think that we are the only ones with insecurities and blemishes and that, therefore, if others come to know our most authentic selves, they will be repulsed. Quite the opposite happens. We discover that we have much in common, and we develop a deep respect for our differences. From a distance, our differences may seem odd and distorted. But as we come to know one another, we understand the context from which differences come. Feelings of respect emerge.

Nothing creates disciples like intimate prayer. This is not primarily the private prayer of the disciple nor the public prayer of the congregation. Rather, the prayer that truly transforms is the small-group prayer. In the intimate prayer circle we are prayed for specifically and individually, and we pray by name for others. The prayer of clichés or the stylized prayer has no meaning here. As disciples become vulnerable before one another and God, they pray at the hurting and growing edges of their lives. Prayer is one of the best methods of accountability between persons and with God.

Prayer has two roles within the intimate Christian group. First, it helps us to listen. A small discipleship group can trust one another enough not only to allow silence, but also to use the silence to listen for the Spirit. In nearly any other setting, silence causes us discomfort. Yet it is in silent waiting that the Spirit of God most effectively shapes and molds us.

Second, in intimate prayer we are seeking. We are seeking for ourselves and seeking on behalf of one another. A whole new chapter on intercessory prayer is written in intimacy.

Nothing holds us more accountable to growth than does intimate prayer with a few Christian friends whom we respect and love. We can voice our concerns and recognize that the prayers that follow will carry the touch of healing.

In Summary

We began the chapter stating that every church needs to be an including community. However, churches can become stretched out of shape if they do not recognize that there must be some limits to their inclusiveness. Inclusive churches use the diversity of their membership to undergird the tension of transformational growth. Exclusive churches use the conformity of their members to undergird unity.

The very act of including is an act of discipleship. To include is one function of the call of discipleship. It is the act of inviting and sustaining persons on a faith journey. Inclusive churches are prepared for renewal as they discover the points at which inclusion and discipleship are complementary.

The four words of renewal for inclusive churches begin with a call to focus our congregations upon discipleship as we grow in accountability, in respect, and in intimacy. As they embody these four words of renewal, inclusive churches will become communities of disciples committed to a more radical obedience to Jesus Christ.

5

The Inclusive Church as a Community of Disciples

Discipleship in the inclusive church presents a problem. It is the nature of this problem to which this book is addressed. If we are to take discipleship seriously in the inclusive church, we might assume that we will be forced to make an artificial response or a painful compromise. We think of discipleship as restrictive and demanding, while the atmosphere of the inclusive church is generally casual and tolerant. Yet, this superficial analysis is subject to distortion. A more in-depth probe and review of the nature of discipleship and the inclusive church is necessary.

The Nature of Discipleship

Discipleship to Jesus Christ demands discipline and obedience. It requires a process of faithful transformation until each person becomes "an altogether new creature" in Christ (Galatians 6:15, *The Jerusalem Bible*). However, discipleship to Christ is characterized best, not by its restrictions, but by describing it as a liberating experience in the world, in the life of the believer, and in the community of faith. Discipleship does not emphasize the doors it closes but rather the doors it opens. "When Christ freed us, he meant us to remain free. Stand firm, therefore, and do not submit again to the yoke of slavery" (Galatians 5:1, *The Jerusalem Bible*). We enter into discipleship in order that Christ may free us. Discipleship is never imposed on us by Christ and need not be imposed on us by the church or its leaders. The choice to be a disciple is voluntary, and each fork in the journey toward the fullness of Christ is a point for our own free decision.

Discipleship in the exclusive church is the process of imitation. Synonyms for "imitate" are "copy," "mimic," "duplicate," "repeat," and "replicate." In light of this interpretation, the object of discipleship is to repeat Jesus' life in new times and places. As imitators of Christ, members of exclusive churches reach for a common interpretation of Christ, which all strive to attain. This approach to Christian discipleship is not without problems.

> The following of Jesus does not come down to the mere imitation of Jesus. First of all, it is in fact impossible to do exactly what he himself did. Second and even more important, the Christian should not "imitate" Jesus precisely because an intrinsic and essential feature of Jesus' own moral course is its localization in history. . . . Christians must accept the moral responsibility of determining how to situate themselves concretely in history. . . .
>
> Discipleship is not imitation, therefore; and neither is it a reproduction of certain historical traits of Jesus.[1]

The inclusive church views discipleship growth as transformation. The exclusive church views discipleship growth as conformation. The inclusive church presumes that becoming like Christ means discovering the unfolding presence of Christ. The exclusive church presumes that becoming like Christ means discovering the unchanging model of Christ.

Inclusive churches view transformational growth as the way in which disciples creatively become new persons in Christ. They affirm that what it means to be "in Christ" is linked to the historical Jesus, yet unique to each person and to each era. Exclusive churches view conformational growth as the way in which disciples imitate Christ. They affirm that Christ is a universal and unchanging model to which they are called to conform.

The point to be made is that discipleship growth need not be a process of *conformity*. This is the way of the exclusive church, but it is not the only legitimate approach. Discipleship growth can be a process of *transformation*, in which each person becomes a "new person" in Christ Jesus (see Romans 12:2 and Ephesians 4:23).

> The expression, "creative discipleship," sounds initially somewhat paradoxical. If persons become disciples they allow themselves to be determined by the one they follow. They imitate their leader, but they are not themselves creative. This impression is false, however. Discipleship . . . is not imitation. . . . Jesus did not call his disciples to imitate him but to participate in his messianic mission: "Preach as you go, saying, 'The kingdom of heaven is at hand.' Heal the sick, raise the dead, cleanse lepers, cast out demons." (Matt. 10:7f) They are not called upon to help

him carry his cross, but to take up their own cross (Matt. 10:38). The call to discipleship is therefore a call to responsible maturity in fellowship—yes, even friendship—with Jesus.[2]

If we do not view discipleship as imitation, then discipleship can be creative. We will not then be invited to be imitators of Jesus but followers of Christ. "Followers" implies that the journey of faith continues. It did not conclude with the death of Jesus upon a cross. It continues in the lives of the followers of Christ today. To be a follower involves the creative task of *coming together* in new times and places, *coming to Christ* as we experience his ongoing leadership, and *coming to our most authentic selves*, as we *listen imaginatively* and *with discernment* for how Christ is calling us *to act and obey*. This is an uncharted journey for which there are no maps.

If discipleship is not imitative, then we can accept the variety of its expressions. If discipleship is not imitative, then it offers choices. If it is not imitative, then an imaginative response to Christ is required. If it is not imitative, then we will each be called to a different role. We will talk and act in unique ways; we will experience Christ distinctively.

Disciples are invited to be citizens of a kingdom of heaven on earth, which Jesus inaugurated. The gifts we bring and the avenues of service within the kingdom are many. "There are many dwelling-places in my Father's house; if it were not so I should have told you . . ." (John 14:2, NEB).

If disciples can be characterized by variety, by the creativity of our response, and by the way we listen with our imaginations, then inclusive churches can naturally approach the biblical meaning of discipleship.

The Inclusive Church

Inclusive churches themselves are the other dimension of the problem. Inclusive churches cannot be centers of discipleship if they are also centers of tolerance. Tolerance, as opposed to respect, encourages distance between persons and the privacy of faith.

Inclusive churches often emphasize an openness in which accountability is viewed as an intrusion into privacy, a sacrifice of acceptance, and a violence against personal freedom. These churches can be so casual and laissez-faire as to be unable to encourage any self-discipline or discipline among members. In inclusive churches we often find a lukewarm faith.

What we are seeking for in inclusive churches is a position between their tendency toward a highly individualistic faith and the exclusive churches' model of conformity. This balance will be found as inclusive churches emphasize a process in which they seek creative discipleship.

The highly individualistic church that can affirm nothing but its own plurality is not built upon personal freedom, as has been supposed, but upon license. Freedom is always gained within limits and is always accompanied by responsibility. In too many inclusive churches, the casual atmosphere gives permission for plurality to exist for its own sake, rather than giving freedom to persons to discover their unique call to grow in Christ.

In the previous chapter, we described the four words of renewal that offer a style of inclusiveness that can enhance discipleship to Christ. If inclusive churches place a priority on commitment to discipleship, if they encourage mutual accountability, if respect for persons and differences is evidenced, and if intimacy emerges, then these churches are poised to prepare persons for creative discipleship to Christ. I do not mean to imply that transforming inclusive churches into discipleship communities will be easy. The changes for which we are calling will not happen overnight. The first step is to envision the transformed church to which Christ is calling.

The Inclusive Church as a Community of Disciples

A vision must be created for the inclusive church as a community of disciples. It is a vision that must describe the future direction of growth and lure those in the inclusive church into the new reality. There are at least four necessary dimensions to this vision:

1. *An inclusive church needs an atmosphere in which persons are encouraged to grow as disciples of Jesus Christ.* The atmosphere encourages growth; it does not require or dictate it. Members of these churches will experience the feeling of encouragement as the worth of discipleship is lifted up in the church's worship, study, service, and fellowship. The focus of the church will cause persons to gravitate toward discipleship. To encourage is not to trick, to be devious, or to induce guilt. To encourage is to invite. Encouragement is the initiatory action of the church to invite persons to take discipleship seriously. Persons are invited to discover the fullness that is Jesus Christ. The atmosphere itself can encourage and invite persons to open the door.

2. *An inclusive church needs to provide opportunities for discipleship growth for those who seek it.* This is the responsive action. In the stages

of life there are seasons appropriate for reassessment, challenge, and growth, and there are seasons of life appropriate for contentment and rest. Adults pass in and out of such seasons. We do not intend to create an artificial climate in which, throughout their lifetimes, adults are frantically working at the task of discipleship.

One of the most interesting things our church learned was that when persons in small groups were asked during the year to assess an obstacle to discipleship in their lives, many discovered that they were confronting the same obstacle each time. Basically, they were continually working on the same agenda. Perhaps by the end of the year they better understood the problem, although the focus might have changed somewhat. But they were living with the same dilemma throughout the year. This is typical of the adult life cycle. Sometimes adults experience change with such force and rapidity that it makes adolescence appear tranquil. But more often, growth for adults occurs gradually. In fact, it is generally true that the more gradual the change, the more trustworthy and dependable it is.

At the seeking seasons of our lives, opportunities for discipleship growth need to be available. We can encourage persons to engage in discipleship growth opportunities, but in the inclusive church, *they* decide when the time is right. And just because the time is right for one person does not mean that the time is right for another.

In an inclusive church it is better to offer a variety of opportunities that require different commitments and that give focus to complementary dimensions of discipleship.

3. *An inclusive church needs a discipleship plan that continuously lifts up adult discipleship as an active priority in the church's decision making and planning.* If discipleship is important, then it must be planned and given priority. This is an activity that must be shared with the broadest possible cross section of the church's leadership. I advocate the adoption and implementation of a discipleship plan that describes for each church an environment of encouragement, the invitation to discipleship, and the opportunities for growth available. This discipleship plan should consider that those entering the faith journey will be different from those continuing it. The inward and outward dimensions of discipleship should be encouraged in the plan. The plan should be an active part of the ongoing agenda of the appropriate decision-making bodies in the church. All new members should receive the plan and an interpretation of it. The discipleship plan needs to keep in mind the

congregation's inclusiveness and the variety that exists within it.

4. *An inclusive church needs to use its diversity to inspire creative discipleship and to discover personal freedom within a framework of mutual accountability.* This dimension colors the other parts of the vision. Mutual, voluntary accountability is the discipline needed in the inclusive church to hold us to the course of discipleship growth. One person in our church said of a recent discipleship-group experience, "I realized that I have failed and disappointed my family and friends. Yet there is hope and renewal even in failure. There is growth in pain. There is support from my discipleship group for the changes which must now be made." This person was voluntarily turning to a small group of fellow disciples for the accountability to hold him to a path of admitted difficulty.

Jesus was fully aware of the cost of discipleship, for he told the parable of the grain of seed that must be buried in the ground and "die" before it can begin to bear fruit. Another group participant said, "When I think of discipleship, I think of cost. Discipleship costs. And I have to think whether I want to pay the cost." That is the thought of every serious disciple.

By entering into mutual, voluntary accountability, we grow in the personal freedom found in Jesus Christ. We discover our most authentic selves. The diversity of the inclusive church need not dictate a watered-down form of discipleship. It need not imply a casual attitude toward Christian commitment. Discerning Christ's unique call may require that we count the cost of discipleship by some measure other than conformity to an external source of authority.

The inclusive church can value its diversity as a resource for discipleship growth. The diversity can challenge narrow assumptions, inspire creative discipleship, personalize the cost of Christ's call, and broaden our view of the reconciling activity of Christ in our lives and in the world. Because the goal in the inclusive church is not conformity, disciples can be *transformed* as new persons in Christ. This does not occur through individualistic insight but through a process of mutual accountability. Contrary to the fear of many, discipleship will not diminish but will enhance the integrity of the inclusive church.

In small, accountable groups in the inclusive church, we seek to join together a diverse cross section of age, sex, theological stance, race, life-style, or whatever diversity is available. We challenge disciples to use this diversity as they grow through one another toward Jesus Christ.

Criteria to Determine Discipleship Growth Opportunities in the Inclusive Church

We can now summarize the criteria offered in this book for planning discipleship growth opportunities in the inclusive church. *The opportunities need to offer:*

1. Discipleship growth that emphasizes a continual transformation into the image of Christ. Discipleship is not a one-time event.

2. The death-resurrection paradigm as a model of how disciples grow. This needs to be evident, though certainly not explicit, in each growth opportunity.

3. Help for disciples as they discover who they are in light of Christ and find the nature of their calling and ministry.

4. An environment in which participants can come together, come to Christ, come to their most authentic selves.

5. An environment in which participants can listen, using their imaginations and intellects, for the direction of Christ's leading.

6. An environment in which the action of discipleship in the participants' life-styles and in the world is encouraged, nurtured, and evaluated.

7. Mutual accountability for growth.

8. Intimacy among participants.

9. Respect among participants.

10. A focus on the biblical word as participants learn from the text and allow the text to speak to them.

11. A focus upon intimate prayer with others, in which participants listen for God and seek God's will.

12. A balance between the journey inward and the journey outward, the inclusive nature of discipleship.

The Vision Embodied

Much of what has been shared here has been learned from only one inclusive church as it has focused upon discipleship growth. I am convinced that fertile ground remains at the juncture of inclusive churches and Christian discipleship growth. The issues are huge and we have only scratched the surface. Much remains to be learned.

The four dimensions of the vision of the inclusive church as a community of disciples are equally important. They each require careful efforts of planning and implementation. An inclusive church can take discipleship growth seriously if it has a conducive atmosphere, if it provides specific opportunities for growth, it if makes discipleship growth an integral part of its planning and decision making, and if it finds ways to use its diversity to inspire creative discipleship.

Can an inclusive church base its corporate life upon obedience to Christian discipleship? It makes no sense to underestimate the cost of adult discipleship growth. Growing as disciples requires of us a radical letting-go before we can enjoy the harvest of Christ embodied in our lives. Jesus tells us what is expected of those who would be his disciples (see John 12:24). This text also suggests what must occur within churches that seek to take Jesus' style of discipleship seriously. What is called for is not the death of diversity but the death of a casual approach to faith that is neither disturbed nor excited by Jesus' radical call. When the inclusive church takes up this cross and follows, perhaps the most creative discipleship in our day will emerge.

6

Resources for Adult Discipleship Growth

This chapter contains descriptions of three of the resources that were developed for use as one inclusive church attempted to become a community of disciples. The following resources are included in this chapter (additional discipleship resources, including the second, third, and fourth year leader's guide for the small discipleship groups, may be obtained by writing directly to Discipleship Resources, c/o the First Baptist Church, 111 W. Monument, Dayton, OH 45402):

1. A description of the small discipleship groups and a copy of the leader's guide for the first year

2. The Adult Discipleship Plan of the First Baptist Church of Dayton, Ohio

3. A description of the New Creation Fellowship, which incorporates and acquaints new and prospective members with the life of the First Baptist Church of Dayton

These resources are included here to encourage adult discipleship growth in local churches. The user of the book is granted permission to reproduce pages from this chapter, as needed, to educate or nurture persons in the local Christian community. Such copies are not to be sold, and proper credit must be included on each reproduction.

Programs and experiences will need to be tailored to meet each specific situation. The investment of personal creativity is always beneficial. The material here is presented to be used, adapted, and tailored to meet the needs of local churches who want to provide growth opportunities in adult discipleship. In nearly all cases, these resources were developed in a collaborative effort by members and pastors of the First Baptist Church of Dayton.

Small Discipleship Groups

There are three purposes for the small discipleship groups: (a) to develop an intimate, accountable atmosphere of respect in a small-group expression of the body of Christ; (b) to stimulate one another in growth toward Christ and in ministry in the world; and (c) to explore, at a more profound level, personal meanings of Christian discipleship.

The small discipleship groups meet biweekly for twelve to fifteen sessions. We begin the groups each year in September. Nine to eleven participants form one group. We divide the year into three-session units and concentrate upon one biblical passage in each triad. All groups meet in the church building on Sunday evenings for two-hour sessions. In forming the groups, we attempt to include in each group the broadest cross section possible. The inclusiveness of the groups is based upon sex, age, marital status, theological stance, and tenure of church members. Groups also try to involve urban and suburban dwellers and persons with various levels of experience in group participation skills. Each participant is given a journal in which to record new learnings and insights throughout the year.

Each group has co-leaders, and this is one of the most successful components of the small groups. Most of our leaders begin with no experience. The small-group leaders meet together in a leaders' group on the weeks when the small groups are not meeting. The leader session is a sharing group also, with the specific focus upon training. During the beginning leader sessions, the co-trainers of this group offer a rationale for discipleship groups and identify good leadership behaviors.

During the fall, the trainers lead the leaders' group in the same exercises that the leaders will use the next week with their groups. Modeling is the primary training method. After the leaders feel more comfortable with their roles, the leaders' group evaluates the process, shares problem situations, gives input for upcoming session designs, and provides ongoing personal support for one another.

Membership in the groups is subject to the covenant that each group creates at the beginning of the year. The covenants generally emphasize participation, spiritual disciplines through the week, and confidentiality.

On occasion, all the groups meet together for a portion of a session.

Fellowship meals or group closings are typical forms for these total-group sessions.

The groups are more than sharing groups; they are discipleship groups. In order to focus upon this, we developed a model using a three-session unit. In each triad we focus upon one passage of Scripture. We choose biblical texts that reveal an important message about Christian discipleship. In the first year we used texts from the Gospels. However, in subsequent years we have used Old Testament facts, as well as passages from Paul's letters. In each of the three sessions, we explore the passage from a different approach. (See page 86 for a diagram of this approach.)

First Session: We attempt *to connect our personal stories with the Bible's story.* We sometimes distribute a four-page leaflet entitled "My Story and the Bible's Story." The first page attempts to help the participants apply the major themes of the biblical passage to their daily experiences. For example, in the story of Jesus and his disciples in Gethsemane, the front page of this leaflet helps the readers to explore their personal experience with such issues as sleep, failure and disappointment, ability to confront others, and so on. The second page of the leaflet asks participants to read the related passage in the Bible. The third page attempts to form a synthesis between the personal stories revealed on page 1 and the Bible's story. The last page encourages a daily prayer discipline related to the theme and a quotation for further reflection. We do not use this leaflet in every triad, but the purpose of the session remains the same.

Second Session: We often use a guided meditation to allow the biblical story to speak to each participant. We begin by urging participants to relax, often through breathing exercises. Through our imaginations, we attempt to allow the Holy Spirit to guide us in an encounter with Christ, trying to be open to a word, a message, or a visual image. After these guided meditations, we urge participants to use their journals to record their experiences and then to share this with a partner or the total group.

Third Session: We sometimes use a "death and resurrection" paradigm in an attempt to be held accountable to the truth as well as the particular calling of the biblical text. We often distribute a worksheet on which participants are asked to summarize their learnings from the first and second sessions, as well as any other insights they have had while "living with" the passage for the previous weeks. Participants are asked to identify the "death" to which Christ is calling them, what Christ is calling them to surrender. Then they are to identify from this the new life, or resurrection, to which Christ is leading them. Finally, they apply this learning to the everyday world. What impact does this have on their ministry or opportunities for service? Even in those sessions when we don't use the words "death" and "resurrection," the object of the session is for group members to be held accountable to the text and to the call of God.

The three-session approach is primarily an eisegetical approach to the Scripture. Most people neither understand nor have experienced this approach. It is not a study about the passage but is an opportunity for people to listen to Christ through the passage and to recognize how it intersects with their daily lives.

The exegetical approach, a study of the passage in context, is often offered by a sermon preached in the Sunday-morning service, based upon the text and related to the group experience. We prepare exegetical materials to complement the main thrust of the sessions. Sometimes these result in group exercises and other times in take-home exercises.

In the typical group session, a getting-started activity reestablishes an atmosphere of trust, respect, and intimacy. Then we engage in the discipleship model. At the conclusion of each session, we plan a time of affirmation, sharing of personal concerns and joys, and group prayer. Often we use the seasons of the church year as foci for the sessions.

Here is a typical session outline:
A. Getting-started exercise, sharing of concerns and celebrations
B. Discipleship model based upon a biblical text
C. Group closing and prayer

As we went through our first year with these small groups, we recognized a tendency for this triad approach to become repetitive. We discovered that a great deal of time was spent sitting and discussing. We began to introduce exercises that would get participants involved with their hands and bodies. We have found that a mixture of experiences that are familiar as well as serendipitous is the most effective. Detailed descriptions of each session in our first year are included later in this chapter.

The testimony to the value of these groups, in terms of discipleship growth, was offered by participants in a survey taken before and after the groups. One participant said prior to the groups, "I have some reservations about this group. I am not sure I want to reveal as much of myself as I think this type of group will demand." At the conclusion this person said, "I feel that I have more to offer than I had believed before. I am less fearful."

Another person said at the beginning of the year,

At this point I feel pretty inadequate. After our first session, it seems like everyone has so many more "religious" experiences to draw from than me [sic]. It seems that I don't have much to talk about; I don't have anything to give the group.

At the end of the year, she said, "This group has been a catalyst to make me examine my own faith and work towards making it a more personal experience." Still another person said,

At first I thought discipleship meant evangelism and knocking on doors and witnessing to people; but now I don't think it necessarily has to be that overt. It's being Christlike to others and doing it not for your own self, but because you love God and love what Christ is doing in your life. You want that for others.

Another participant said at the conclusion of the groups,

Placing myself in the guided meditations has been difficult, but it has made me realize that God's words and examples can be guides for living each day. This practice has opened my eyes and imagination and expanded the knowledge the Bible can bring into my personal life.

And finally,

This experience has made the terms "discipleship" and "journey" more than just catch phrases. At this point and time, I have made a more complete commitment than ever before to be part of a growing Christian journey.

From our evaluation of the small discipleship groups, we learned these things:

1. *The death/resurrection paradigm is difficult for many persons to comprehend or apply to their lives.* For most of us, crucifixion and resurrection are events in the life of Jesus, not in our own lives. Many participants felt that using the death/resurrection paradigm in four sessions through the year caused them to repeat themselves. Regardless of the text, when asked to apply this concept to their lives, they discovered that the same life issues kept being repeated. On the other hand, some people reported that being held accountable by the biblical text and by their group was challenging and many simply didn't like it. We discovered that many people didn't like pulling together the

learnings of the previous sessions and being "forced" to look at what this means for their lives. We enjoy dealing in generalities.

2. *In some triads, the exegetical dimension was weak.* To have the pastor preach a sermon on the passage as the groups are exploring it is a good thing to do, but it cannot be the only exegetical input. We recognize that when some say they want Bible study they have in mind a safe, information-oriented approach in which they can amass biblical facts, names, and places. Living with a passage and allowing Christ to speak through its story was challenging at the first of the year. Many people came to appreciate this model as the year concluded. More study about the passage, its context and meaning, would have been helpful, particularly if it had occurred in the sessions themselves. To have included other related biblical materials would also have enhanced the approach. Our participants were interested in the exegetical approach to the texts.

3. *The three-session sequence ("My Story and the Bible's Story," the guided meditation, and the death/resurrection paradigm) was appreciated by many.* It introduced a more novel approach to the Scriptures than had been anticipated. It is important to begin the first triad of the year with a passage that is easily comprehensible. The guided meditation was perhaps the least appreciated at the first of the year and the most appreciated by the end. A number of people learned to free their imaginations to act as an avenue for the Spirit.

While the intent of the three-session sequence was affirmed, we learned that more variety in the way it was developed would have made the process less repetitive. However, for some participants, the repetition was a source of security.

4. *The leaders' group was essential to the validity of the participants' groups.* It was not a frill, nor simply desirable, for the first year of experimentation; it was a necessity. As more leaders gain small group experience, the nature of this training group changes. But the support gained here and the congruence of the groups that occurred in this setting was crucial. The concept of having co-leaders was affirmed by leaders and participants.

5. *The covenantal nature of the groups was strongly affirmed.* People appreciated the intimacy, the accountability, the trust, and the interpersonal support. The ministry of prayer within the groups was a powerful presence. The groups seemed to be graced by the ability to pray for one another by name and by specific concern. Accountability slowly developed within most groups. Some groups developed little

mutual accountability, while others were able to nurture this. Even though the groups are together for only one year, the returning participants who join new groups the following fall undoubtedly bring a readiness to enter into mutual accountability more quickly and at a more profound level.

6. *The format of the small groups was affirmed by the participants.* Meeting every other week on Sunday evenings with the same group was appreciated. For all the groups to meet at the same place and time was a source of encouragement to the groups and prevented them from feeling isolated. The occasional total-group sessions introduced another level of legitimate interaction.

7. *We urged groups to include personal and group devotional disciplines in their covenant that would extend beyond the sessions.* Often these were daily times of praying for other members of the group or a commitment to "live with" the biblical passage being explored in the sessions. In most groups, this covenant was taken seriously at first but decreased in priority through the year. Many of the participants felt this deterioration was a weakness. More accountability to personal disciplines would have been welcomed.

8. *Whenever a new approach to something as basic as the Bible is being initiated, the introduction is important.* A careful description is needed of what will happen, what people can expect, and what will be asked of them.

9. *The freedom of participants to come to their own conclusions and to discover the creativity of discipleship was appreciated.* The opportunity to learn with and from those with different faith positions was affirmed. We found that the inclusiveness of our church, as it was experienced within the small discipleship groups, was one of the features most highly prized by the participants. Many described someone whom they had never understood, liked, or trusted, and for whom they now had deeper appreciation. They may still not agree, but mutual agreement was not the goal. Respect for inclusiveness was the result.

10. *The biblical approach called upon people to use their imaginations as they recognized connections between the reality of their everyday world and the reality of the Bible.* While this required a risk, in nearly all the groups people expressed appreciation for this challenge.

In short, we discovered many things we would improve, but overall, the discipleship model accomplished much of what we hoped it would. It helped participants reflect upon the meaning of discipleship in the context of our inclusive church.

Leader's Guide for Small Discipleship Groups: First Year

(Group resources written by Stephen Jones and Karen Tye)

Session 1: Introductory Time

Getting Started: What's in a Name?

Welcome and introductions. Ask the group members to share information about their names: Were they named after anyone? Do they like their name? Does it mean anything? Have they had nicknames? Do they know why their name was selected? Information can be sought about first, middle, and last names.

Sharing fears and expectations. In pairs, ask the participants to share the expectations and fears that they have as they enter these discipleship groups.

The focus of a discipleship group. Explain the purposes of the discipleship group: (a) to develop an intimate atmosphere of respect and accountability in a small-group expression of the body of Christ; (b) to stimulate one another in growth toward Christ and in ministry in the world; and (c) to explore, at a more profound level, personal meanings of Christian discipleship.

Hand out a personal journal to each participant. Urge the participants to use their journals throughout the year and to bring them and their Bibles to each session. The journal is more than a place to store information for the small group. It is a place to reflect, to record ideas and feelings, to journalize. The personal journals are three-ring binders, with side pockets for participants to use in keeping handouts.

Urge the participants to make the discipleship group a high priority for this year and to consider the meaning of a small group covenant. A covenant-writing activity will be included in the next session.

Group Exercise: Who Has Been Christ in Your Life?

Offer this explanation:

These are discipleship groups, designed to help nurture us as adults to grow in our faith and understanding of God, and to see Christ alive and at work in us and in the world.

Jesus' goal with his disciples was to move them beyond being just imitators to being like him in the world, bearers of God's love. Jesus modeled for them what life was to be like and constantly challenged them to grow. When they were afraid to risk, he supported them to do even greater things. He kept modeling and challenging.

That is how we learn as disciples . . . by watching the people around us, seeing them in action, having models. Tonight, we want to look back through our lives and recognize some of the models we have had, particularly those people who have modeled Christ.

On a sheet of paper have participants make four columns with the following headlines: *Children, Adolescence, Young Adulthood,* and *Adulthood.* Under each of these headings, participants should list the persons who modeled Christlike behavior during that period of their lives. Under each person's name, have group members list those characteristics or actions that caused this person to be chosen.

Ask the participants to share this list with another person and then with the total group, responding to these questions: "What did you learn from this exercise?" "Were there any surprises?" "How does this challenge your own discipleship journey?"

Closing Exercise: Sharing Concerns and Prayer

Throughout the year, encourage a sharing of personal concerns at the conclusion of the sessions. This is an opportunity to share the hurts and joys of daily living in an atmosphere of prayerful support. This provides the group the opportunity to pray for one another in specifics rather than in generalities.

Also, encourage the role of silence in group prayer times. Too often, persons are uncomfortable with silence, feeling the need to say something to fill the empty space. But silence need not be empty. Silence can be an opening for the Spirit of God to speak to individuals or to small groups. Small groups can use the silence to develop an ability to listen and interpret the activity of the Spirit in their midst.

Small group prayer in these sessions will most often be a "season of prayer," combining silence with random, verbal, and voluntary intercessory prayers by the participants. Verbal prayers can express support among group participants, but no person is pressured to pray verbally.

Close the session with a sharing of concerns and a "season of prayer."

Session 2: Introductory Time

Getting Started: Describe Yourself

Urge the participants to look back over their past week and decide which one of these items characterizes their experience: *dancing shoes, house slippers,* or *combat boots.* Group members are to explain why the symbolic description corresponds to their past week.

Group Exercise: Covenant Making

In this session, participants will create a covenant that will guide their group life and reflect the commitment they desire to make to one another: What does this group agree to do together? What practices or disciplines do they want to adopt while together or apart? In what ways can this group be supportive of one another?

Some suggestions for covenants would be:

● Attendance and punctuality at each group session (group members are responsible for informing one of the leaders if absence is necessary).

● Confidentiality (what other persons share in the group is not discussed beyond the group but participants can, of course, feel free to discuss what they themselves have shared in the group; the purpose of this is not to create a closed, secretive group, but to develop trust).

● Freedom of participation (participants can decide whether or not to become involved in each exercise of the group without coercion or guilt).

● Disciplines of prayer and devotion (do the group members want to pray for each other regularly or daily? Is there a discipline of prayer and spiritual devotion to which participants want to be held accountable by the group?).

● Journalizing (keeping a personal journal in which to record experiences and ideas relevant to discipleship growth).

Urge the group members to decide upon a covenant and have them write it in their journals. A time should be established to evaluate how the covenant is working. They should record this date in their journals as well.

Group Exercise: Trust Walk

Share this background with your group in your own words:

We are embarking on a yearlong spiritual journey together. As prepared as we may be for that journey and no matter how much we may want to take it, we still begin the journey with anxiety and fear. There is risk in taking any trip or journey. We don't know what lies ahead or what detours, roadblocks, hazards we may face. It takes courage to journey. It takes trust in ourselves, in each other, and in God.

I want us to look for a few minutes at the issue of trust and to share in an exercise of trust. But first, let's read together a Scripture about trust: Matthew 14:22-32.

The disciples were on a journey, a new road for them. And often they didn't understand all that was happening to them. But they were asked to trust, to believe that Jesus was a good guide. We, too, are being asked to trust, to trust our guides: Scripture, one another, and God.

To help us to get in touch with some of our struggles with trust, I want us to take a trust walk. I couldn't manage a lake, so this building will have to do! Pick one partner and take turns keeping your eyes closed as the other guides you through the church helping you to "see" without eyes. The only stipulation is that this be done nonverbally, with no talking. Take five minutes for one person to be the guide and the other the blind person; then switch, allowing five minutes in reversed roles. Come back to this room for sharing at the close of your walk.

Upon their return, discuss these questions:

a. What did you learn about yourself and trust?
b. Do you see any similarities and/or differences between yourself and Peter in this Scripture (Matthew 14:22-32)? Between yourself and Jesus?

The questions can be discussed in pairs and then with the total group.

Group Exercise: Guided Meditation

Guide the group through this experience:

On a regular basis through the course of this year we will be sharing in some meditative experiences together. Meditation is an ancient discipline of the church that twentieth-century Christians are beginning to rediscover.

To me meditation is practice *for* prayer. It is an inward journey when for a few moments we get "out of our heads" and down into our center, to that deeper well of wisdom where God resides within us. As C. S. Lewis says, meditation is the act of "following the sunbeam back up to the sun"—of tracing our stream of energy to its source.

Meditation is an important tool to use on our journey and can help us learn some truths we need to know. There is no right or wrong way to meditate. We won't get hung up on technique. Relaxation and the use of your imaginations, are two basic tools. You remember your imagination—that thing you were supposed to leave behind in childhood? But as Jesus says—unless we become like children. Need I say more?

Let us begin our initial experience together by clearing our laps of any materials and find a comfortable sitting position. Perhaps some of you would be more comfortable lying on the floor; feel free to do so. Close your eyes and become aware of your breathing. Begin to take deeper breaths, pulling in clean air and slowly exhaling air containing tensions. Continue breathing slowly and deeply saying to yourself, *relax*. Begin to feel the tension leave your body. Breath slowly—relax—let go. Quietly let your breathing settle into a pattern that is comfortable for you.

In your mind's eye, imagine you are standing by a large lake. Look at the water; note its deep blue color. Watch the waves hitting the shore. Become aware of your surroundings by the lake. It is quiet and peaceful. Enjoy it for a moment. (*Pause.*) In the distance you see a boat. It is rowing toward you. When it reaches shore you notice the people in it. Who are they? (*Pause.*) They ask you to come for a ride, and you accept. You get into the boat, and they begin to row back out to the center of the lake. You are enjoying the ride when you notice that it is turning dark and the waves are picking up. A storm has come up suddenly. You begin to feel afraid, the panic begins to rise in the boat. Can you reach the shore without being overturned? The fear rises. Suddenly you hear a voice say, "Courage! It is I. Do not be afraid!" You look up and see Jesus walking toward you across the water. What are your thoughts? (*Pause.*) He motions to you to come to him. What do you do? What are your feelings? What happens? (*Pause.*) Then you realize that you are back on shore again and it is time to leave. You say good-by and walk slowly away pondering what has happened. (*Pause.*) Slowly you become aware you are in this room, and when you are ready, open your eyes.

Closing Exercise: Affirmation Circle

Distribute the handout entitled "Affirm One Another." (See the next page.) The group will read the passage from Romans in unison and then focus upon one person in the group at a time and invite the other members to affirm this person verbally. An affirmation is a specific statement to that person lifting up something that you appreciate about them or calling forth a Christlike quality that you recognize in that person. After a period of affirmation, the leader will close attention on the person by stating his or her name; then the group will respond, "We affirm you, as Christ affirms us." Then the group will focus on the next person until all have been affirmed.

A brief closing prayer will conclude the session.

Session 3: First in the Galilee Triad

Getting Started: Your Weather Report

Ask the participants to describe their week as if it were a weather report, such as, *partly cloudy, overcast skies,* a *sunshiny day, lightning storms followed by haze,* and so on.

Discipleship Exercise

Describe to the group the discipleship model to be used during this yearlong experience. It is important for leaders to be thoroughly familiar with the approach and with some of the theological rationale behind it.

To assist the group members in interpreting the three-session model, explain the goal of each session.

First Session of the Triad: to connect our personal stories with the Bible's story

Second Session of the Triad: to see ourselves within the Bible's story as the Spirit of Christ speaks to us

Third Session of the Triad: to be held accountable to the text by understanding the death and resurrection to which Christ calls us

Use the handout "An Approach to Discipleship Growth," on page 86.

Affirm One Another

AFFIRM ONE ANOTHER . . . AS CHRIST AFFIRMS YOU.

LIFT UP ONE ANOTHER . . . AS CHRIST LIFTS YOU.

ACCEPT ONE ANOTHER . . . AS CHRIST ACCEPTS YOU.

SCRIPTURAL ADMONISHMENT TOWARD AFFIRMATION:

Let us stop judging one another. Instead, you should decide never to do anything that would make your neighbor stumble or fall into sin.

We must aim always at those things that bring peace and that help strengthen one another.

We should all consider our neighbors and think what is for their good and will build up the common life.

And may God, the source of patience and encouragement, enable you to have the same point of view among yourselves by following the example of Christ Jesus, so that all of you together may praise the God of our Lord Jesus Christ.

Accept one another, then, for the glory of God, as Christ has accepted you. (Romans 14:13,19; 15:2,5,7; *TEV,* adapted).

WE AFFIRM YOU . . . AS CHRIST AFFIRMS US.

Guidelines for the First Session of the Triad

1. *The leader should not tell the participants the Scripture under discussion before distributing "My Story and the Bible's Story."* This will enable a freer response to the first page of this handout.

2. *Urge honesty in filling out "My Story and the Bible's Story."* The more superficial and general this response is, the less helpful it will be to the participant. Take the time to dig for the real meanings.

3. *The papers are confidential.* The participants are to keep them in their personal journals. At no time does anyone but the participant see them. In two more sessions, participants will need this handout again, so it should be brought to each session, along with the journal.

Discipleship Exercise: "My Story and the Bible's Story"

Distribute the handout "My Story and the Bible's Story." (sample follows this session.) Urge participants to use the biblical story as a parable to their lives, rather than as an event that happened thousands of years ago and that has no connection to today. Provide adequate time for the group to complete the handout. Then discuss it in pairs, and finally with the total group. Participants should share with others only as they feel comfortable. Obviously, if important learnings are shared with at least one other person, the benefit will be greater. To verbalize with another person solidifies new learnings and helps another person to hold one accountable.

Closing Exercise: May God Grant You Strength (Group Prayer)

Ask each person to reflect upon the question "In what ways can we pray for you?" and then to identify one or two areas of concern or growth for which they would like prayers. The group's attention will be focused on each person, one at a time.

The leader will say, "Let us pray for (Mary) both verbally and in silence." At the close of a brief "season of prayer" for each person, begin reading the Scripture on the handout reproduced here, which you have distributed beforehand to each participant. Then the group moves to another participant and follows the same sequence.

This exercise concludes the session.

An Approach to Discipleship Growth

Throughout this year, we will approach discipleship growth in a way that is inherently biblical. We will interact with one biblical text for three sessions. We will study the text, live with the story, and attempt to incorporate its meaning into our lives.

A TYPICAL TRIAD

FIRST SESSION
> To recognize connections between the story of my life and the Bible's story.

SECOND SESSION
> To see myself within the story of the Bible;
> To allow the Holy Spirit to guide me in an encounter with Christ.

THIRD SESSION
> To be held accountable to the story;
> To draw together learnings and apply this to my understanding of discipleship and my everyday life.

A Closing Prayer/Dedication

(in unison)

(Name of the person), may God grant you strength and power through the Spirit . . . that through faith, Christ may dwell in your heart in love. . . . May you be strong to grasp, with all God's people, what is the breadth and length and height and depth of the love of Christ, and to know it, though it is beyond knowledge. And so be completely filled with the very nature of God. Amen.

(Adapted from Ephesians 3:16-19, NEB)

My Story and the Bible's Story

Handout Instructions: The material following can be reproduced on four pages as identified in the text. We used a single 8½-by-14-inch sheet with pages 1 and 4 on one side and pages 2 and 3 on the other. The sheet was then folded in the center to make a folder 7 by 8½ inches. The same process can be used with each of the "My Story and the Bible's Story" handouts.

(Page 1)

(PLEASE DO NOT TURN THE PAGE UNTIL COMPLETING THESE QUESTIONS.)

My Story and the Bible's Story

(Answer these questions as honestly as you can. Only you will be seeing your responses. You need to keep this paper in your personal journal.)

1. Do you like to find solutions to your own problems, or is it easy for you to listen to suggestions from others?

2. Are you involved in any endeavors or situations that seem pointless? or fruitless? or unfulfilling?

3. Who are the important persons in your life to whom you truly listen? (You carefully heed these persons' suggestions.)

4. When was the last time you actually changed your life direction? or changed an important dimension of your life? What prompted the change?

5. Do you have any expectations that you could "meet Christ" in your life in a new or deeper way? Why or why not? How?

(Page 2)

A STORY FROM THE BIBLE

Read John 21:1-8.

(Leave rest of page blank for person to write notes.)

Handout

(Page 3)

SYNTHESIS

1. How does your personal story on page 1 interact with the biblical story on page 2? What are the connections?

2. God's Word often breaks into our lives in unexpected and surprising ways. Are there any surprises from God's Word in this exercise?

3. Our lives can be like the field of a farmer. The farmer plants and harvests the same field for many years without replenishing or fertilizing the soil or rotating the crops. Finally the field wears out. Having received no nourishment, it yields a small harvest.

Is there any sense in which this is a parable of your life, or of a certain dimension of your life? Are there overlooked areas of your life that are in need of some nourishment?

(Page 4)

PRAYER AND PERSONAL DISCIPLINE

Over the next seven days, repeat this prayer as often as is meaningful:

"Lord, make me open to your suggestions."

Or feel free to write your own short prayer for daily use:

FOR YOUR REFLECTION

Every time you make a choice you are turning the central part of you, the part that chooses, into something a little different from what it was before. And taking your life as a whole, with all your innumerable choices, all your life long you are slowly turning this central thing into a creature that is in harmony with God, and with other creatures, and with itself, or else into one that is in a state of war. . . . Each of us at each moment is progressing to the one state or the other.—C. S. Lewis, *Mere Christianity* (New York: Macmillan, Inc., 1943), p. 86.

Session 4: Second in the Galilee Triad

Getting Started: High Point–Low Point

Ask the participants to share a high point and a low point of the previous two weeks since you have met.

Discipleship Exercise: Guided Meditation

Another introduction to meditation is important. Stress the importance of allowing our imagination to lead us. Often our imagination is what we least trust, but it is one of our most reliable guides to the world of the Spirit. The leader will want to stress that in meditation the participant is always in control of his or her own responses, ideas, insights. The leader's role is merely to set the stage for each participant to interact with the Spirit. This is a *trust* exercise! Finally, stress that participants are not "mistreating" Scripture by finding themselves within the story. Indeed, they are making the biblical story come alive in their own experience. They are respecting the biblical story to the point of allowing it to speak to them.

In this spirit of respect and trust, begin the guided meditation.

Guided Meditation—Text: John 21:1-8

We can do meaningful things with our bodies to prepare ourselves for meditation. Sit up, comfortably straight and quiet. Open your hands and lay them, palms up, in your lap, a sign of receptivity.

Breath can be an active symbol of the presence of the Spirit.

Breathe in the presence of God's Spirit. . . .

Breathe out tension, confusion, conflict. . . .

Close your eyes. And let's engage in an exercise of trust. First, you need to trust the leadership of my voice, as I guide you. Sometimes you will follow me closely. . . . Sometimes you will follow your imagination.

And so, second, you must trust your imagination. Your imagination can be a trustworthy guide to open new horizons and new insights. Finally, you must trust the *act of surrender*—

by letting go of worries that clog your thoughts. . . .

by letting go of feelings that clog your imagination. . . .

Let your imagination go . . . follow it . . . as it leads you.

Let us breathe deeply together. . . .

First breathe in . . . deeply . . . then exhale . . . push it out.

Breathe in 1 - 2 - 3 - 4

Release 1 - 2 -·3 - 4

Breathe in relaxation 2 - 3 - 4
Release tension 2 - 3 - 4
Breathe in the Spirit of God . . .
Release and empty yourself . . .
Continue breathing deeply, at a slow, regular pace. (Long pause.)

Imagine yourself in a wooden boat in the middle of a beautiful lake. Notice how clear the water is. Listen to the sounds of the water as it splashes against the sides of your boat. The boat is a familiar, trustworthy place to be. It feels comfortable. Friends are on board with you. Just a few. You recognize them.

You look out over their shoulders to the shores of the lake a distance away. Notice the landscape, the trees . . . bushes . . . rocks . . . hills. . . . You and your friends have been fishing . . . unsuccessfully. Your luck has been discouraging. Actually, you have let the fishing nets dangle on the side of the boat in resignation. It is very still. You and your friends are quiet, each lost in thought. Suddenly you hear a voice from the shore. You turn to see a figure waving at you. His voice echoes across the water.

"Have you caught anything, friends?" he asks. Another in the boats responds with discouragement, "Nothing. The fishing is lousy."

The voice from the shore responds, "Cast your nets on the other side. You'll catch something."

You wonder if he can see a school of fish in the water beside your boat. Has he fished this lake before to know the best spots? How could he know?

You each pull in the large, water-soaked nets. They are completely empty. You cross the boat and dump the nets overboard on the other side. Before the nets reach the water, a school of fish appears, and your nets quickly fill and are bulging with fish. You catch the glimmer in the eye of a nearby friend! You feel the excitement of a big catch! Your blood is flowing. . . .

The nets are so full that you cannot pull them into the boat for fear of breaking them. Two of the friends direct the boat toward shore, toward this mysterious fisherman who directed you to the large catch.

You strain . . . but you cannot recognize the person standing there facing you . . . waiting for you to arrive slowly at the shore. His voice sounds familiar.

Finally, a friend in the boat shouts, "IT IS THE LORD!" You

look again, searching his face, his outstretched hands waiting for you. It *is* the Lord! It *is* Jesus, waiting to see you.

You reach shore. Your feet hit the cold water with a splash as you run to meet him. It is the Lord! It is Jesus, waiting to see you.

Jesus greets all of you, with love and tenderness . . . as friends who have been absent from one another. Jesus directs your friends to drag in the nets and the boat and tend to the fish. You start to help, but Jesus catches your arm. "Can we talk?" he asks. "Talk with me?" you say, startled. You and Jesus find a grassy spot nearby, and he looks at you intently. At first you nervously look away from his quiet stare, but soon you are drawn to his eyes, staring into them, seeing his look of love. Jesus speaks to you, "Do you recall that I asked you to pick up your nets and your discouragement and cast them on the other side of the boat? You obeyed me, and your bounty was great."

Jesus goes on to tell you to consider this a parable for your life: to cast your nets, your life, into new waters; to follow him in a new way; to find a new reservoir of resources he makes available to you; to leave the emptiness, the discouragement, and discover the bounty he offers.

What is Jesus saying to you? Is he asking you for a change in attitude? in faith? in life-style? in action? What is Jesus calling you to do? Listen, now, as he speaks to you (long time of silence.)

You hear what Jesus says and let it soak in. Your time with him is now over. The others have returned from the boat. Jesus gets up and goes off to join them at the shore. Sit alone with your thoughts until you are ready to come back and join us here in this room, sitting together as friends.

Following the meditation, ask participants to write in their personal journals their reflections about their experience and its possible meanings. After this, they can share with a partner and then with the total group.

If there is time, the total group could respond to this question: "Were you able to learn something different from this Scripture and your life than you learned in the previous session?"

It will be important to emphasize that use of the imagination is difficult for many people. To meditate upon Scripture in this way is new to most people. Some sessions will not be as productive as others because participants do not yet know how to meditate, or because the mood of the participant greatly affects meditation.

Closing Exercise: Communion

Holy Communion is the closing exercise, with the elements of bread and wine prepared by the leaders. Read and discuss 1 Corinthians 11:23-26. Ask the participants to serve one another around the circle. Before serving the bread, state how ordinary, everyday, and real bread is to our lives. It is commonplace. Christ took the commonplace and used it as a symbol of the reality of his body, broken for us. As the loaf is passed around the circle, participants may say to each other, "May the word of Christ be as real to you as is this bread."

Then share how necessary and vital it is to have a drink to quench our thirsts. We would not survive without the refreshment of drink. The cup represents the blood of our Lord. It represents the vitality of our Lord, just as a drink of fresh water or juice represents vitality to our lives. As the cup is passed, participants can say to one another, "May the word of Christ be as vital to you as is this cup."

A closing season of prayer can conclude this session.

Session 5: Third in the Galilee Triad

Getting Started

As this session is probably near Thanksgiving, it reflects this theme. In an informal time of sharing, ask the group to respond to this question: "For what are you grateful?"

Discipleship Exercise: The Death-and-Resurrection Paradigm

Using John 12:24, 1 Corinthians 15:36-37, and Romans 6:4-7, introduce the themes of death and resurrection as daily experiences of growth for disciples of Christ. Christ asks that we die so that we might truly live.

Participants in this session will be allowing themselves to be held accountable to the scriptural text by identifying the death and resurrection which they are being called to experience.

Participants will need the following from the previous two sessions: "My Story and the Bible's Story" and their own journal entries in response to the guided meditation. They may also have journal entries written in response to the sermon preached on this text or resulting from their own insights during daily devotion and prayer.

Using these resources, the participants will use the death-and-resurrection-paradigm handout ("Growing into the Full Stature of Christ") to reflect on the meaning of this for their lives. Urge them to deal in specifics and not generalities.

After time is given for individual work, this can be shared with partners and with the total group. Make sure that, as participants share with partners, they are doing this with a variety of the group participants and not always with the same person.

Closing Exercise: Thanksgiving Worship

For a different focus, ask the participants to take the quiz "How Fair Is Fare?" on pages 99-100. Allow a short time for conversation and response following the brief quiz. The point of this thanksgiving focus is not to induce a guilt that cripples us but rather to encourage an awareness, through confession and affirmation, that prompts us to a mature response.

Engage in the time of confession and affirmation following the quiz. Read the quote in unison; then respond in silence before asking for verbal response.

Read the "Thanksgiving Litany," assigning parts as it requests. Sing the hymn "Bread of the World" at the conclusion of the litany.

Have a closing season of prayer.

Answers to the Quiz "How Fair Is Fare?"

1. d	9. d
2. d	10. a
3. a	11. a, b, c, d
4. d	12. c
5. c	13. a
6. c	14. c
7. b	15. c
8. c	

Handout

Growing into the Full Stature of Christ

> *By baptism we were buried with Christ Jesus, and lay dead, in order that, as Christ was raised from the dead . . . so also we might set our feet upon the new path of life.*
>
> *For if we become one with Christ in death, we shall also be one with him in resurrection. We know that the person we once were has been crucified with Christ, for the destruction of the sinful self . . . If we thus died with Christ, we believe that we shall also come to life with him* (Romans 6:4-7, *NEB, adapted*).

A. Read your journal entries from the past two sessions and the related scriptural passage. In the following steps, you will examine these resources in the light of a "death-resurrection" model for discipleship growth.

    MAKE YOUR RESPONSES AS SPECIFIC AS POSSIBLE!

B. **Becoming One with Christ in Death**

    DYING TO THE SINFUL SELF . . .

    From the scriptural passage and your journal responses, can you understand to what God is calling you (to die, to surrender, to let go, to turn away from, to release)?

    Are there obstacles that prevent you from realizing the full stature of Christ?

C. **FOR YOUR REFLECTION**

    "Here stands Christ, in the centre, between me and myself, between the old existence and the new."—Bonhoeffer

    Your hearts and minds must be made completely new, and you must put on the new self, which is created in God's likeness . . . (Ephesians 4:23, *TEV*).

D. **Becoming One with Christ in Resurrection**

PUTTING ON THE NEW SELF . . .   COMING TO NEW
LIFE IN CHRIST . . .

From out of this death, you are being called by God into new life.

What is the specific promise of "resurrection" that God is holding
for you?

E. **Application to Daily Discipleship**

Reflect upon this "death and resurrection" in your life. What
difference will it make in your daily ministry with others?

Will it change how you act as a disciple for Christ? in what ways?

F. As you feel comfortable, share with others in your group.
Dedicate, affirm, support.

How Fair Is Fare?

1. According to the UN Food and Agriculture Organization, nearly _____ people in the world suffer from severe undernutrition—hunger.

a. 50 million
c. 300 million
b. 100 million
d. 500 million

2. There is enough food produced so that everyone could have an adequate diet (3,000 calories per day). Yet millions go hungry. Hunger is caused by _____ .

a. overpopulation
c. unemployment
b. scarcity of food
d. inequitable economic and political relationships

3. Nearly half the world's population, 2 billion people, live on less than $_____ a year.

a. 200   b. 500   c. 750   d. 1,000

4. In Asia, each person consumes about 400 pounds of grain a year. In North America, each person consumes the equivalent of _____ pounds of grain a year, either directly or indirectly in the form of meat and dairy products.

a. 800   b. 1,200   c. 1,600   d. 2,000

5. According to the U.S. Presidential Commission on World Hunger, in the 1970s the gap in food production between rich and poor countries _____ .

a. narrowed slightly
b. stayed about the same
c. widened

6. Of all children, _____ suffer from malnutrition.

a. 5%   b. 10%   c. 25%   d. 50%

7. Every minute, _____ children in the world die of hunger.

a. 4   b. 20   c. 40

8. The consequences of hunger reach beyond food. Diseases such as measles and dysentery, an inconvenience to people in the developed world, can be _____ to people, especially children, already weak from malnutrition.

    a. serious   b. meaningless   c. fatal

9. Inadequate or polluted water sources could be responsible for up to _____ of all sickness and disease, according to the World Health Organization.

    a. 30%   b. 50%   c. 60%   d. 80%

10. If for only half a day all the money spent worldwide on the military could be used to eradicate disease, _____ could be wiped out.

    a. malaria   b. smallpox   c. river blindness

11. Hunger is also related to the allocation of resources. In some countries, the best land is used for crops such as _____ while the poor in those countries go hungry.

    a. coffee   b. sugar   c. cocoa   d. cotton

12. Every day _____ acres of U.S farmland are wasted due to erosion and urban sprawl. This lost land could feed _____ people for a year and produce food worth $1.7 billion to American farmers.

    a. 7,   89,000
    b. 12, 170,000
    c. 34, 260,000

13. According to USDA figures, maximum efficiency, or "economy of scale," in food production is generally achieved by _____ .

    a. one- or two-person farms   b. large corporate farms

14. Hunger in the United States is increasing. Some _____ Americans are living on incomes below the federally established poverty level of $5,900 a year for a family of two ($9,287 for a family of four).

    a. one million   c. 15.7 million
    b. 9.5 million   d. 31.8 million

15. On the basis of the plant protein used to produce meat, _____ most efficiently convert their feed to meat.

    a. grain-fed cattle   b. broiler chickens   c. fish

CHURCH WORLD SERVICE, P.O. Box 968, Elkhart, IN 46515

A SEASON OF THANKSGIVING AMIDST THE REALITY OF THE WORLD

A SEASON OF CONFESSION

"Blessed are you that hunger now, for you shall
be satisfied. . . . Woe to you that are full now,
for you shall hunger" (Luke 6:21,25, RSV).

As you consider your blessings amidst the realities of the world,
toward what confession does this lead you?

Think and pray to yourself, and then share specifically and confessionally with your group.

A SEASON OF AFFIRMATION

A prayer:
Jesus, you are the bread of life, bread broken in order to mend all
broken dreams, broken people, broken homes and hearts. Break
the Good News gently to suffering, struggling spirits, that you are
nourishment to anyone who hungers for life. Amen.

As you consider your blessings amidst the realities of the world,
toward what positive affirmation does this lead you?

Think and pray to yourself, and then share specifically and affirmatively with your group.

Thanksgiving Litany

The following scriptural passages have been selected and compiled to dramatize our dependency on God and one another for that promised daily bread. This reflection invites the participation of five individual readers: The Narrator (N), the Lord (1), humanity in general (2), specific human voices (3), (4), as well as the entire group (All).

N: Thus says the Lord:

1: If you walk in my ways and observe my commandments and do them, then I will give you your rains in their due season, and the land shall yield its increase, and the trees of the field shall yield their fruit. And your threshing shall last to the time of vintage, and the vintage shall last to the time of sowing; and you shall eat your bread to the full, and dwell in your land securely. . . . and I will walk among you, and will be your God, and you shall be my people (Leviticus 26:3-6, 12).

2: You shall eat and be full, and you shall bless the Lord your God for the good land (the Lord) has given you (Deuteronomy 8:10).

1: Come, eat of my bread.

2: Come, eat of my bread.

All: Come, eat of my bread (Proverbs 9:5).

1: Everyone who thirsts, come to the waters; . . . who has no money, come, but and eat (Isaiah 55:1). You shall eat in plenty and be satisfied, and praise the name of the Lord your God (Joel 2:26).

2: Bring forth good from the earth, and wine to gladden the heart, oil to make the face shine, and bread to strengthen the heart (Psalm 104:14-15). Honor the Lord with your substance and with the first fruits of all your produce; then your barns will be filled with plenty, and your vats will be bursting with wine (Proverbs 3:9-10).

1: Come, eat of my bread.

2: Come, eat of my bread.

All: Come, eat of my bread.

2: All living things look hopefully to you and you give them food when they need it (Psalm 145:15-16).

3: You have sown much, and harvested little;

4: You eat, but you never have enough;

3: You drink, but you never have your fill;

Handout

4: You clothe yourselves, but no one is warm.
3: Therefore the heavens about you have withheld the dew,
4: and the earth has withheld its produce (Haggai 1:6, 10).

N: More than 460 million people are permanently hungry. The majority of these are threatened by starvation.

All: Give us this day our daily bread (Matthew 6:11).

N: More than ten million people—most of them under five years of age—will perish this year as a result of too little food.

All: Give us this day our daily bread.

N: The problem is not that there is not enough food to go around. The problem is that enough food does not get around.

All: Give us this day our daily bread.

3: All her people groan as they search for bread;
4: They trade their treasures for food to revive their strength.
3: "Look, O Lord, and behold, for I am despised."
4: Is it nothing to you, all you who pass by?
1: Look and see if there is any sorrow like my sorrow" (Lamentations 1:11-12).

3: What (one) of you, if (your) son asks (you) for bread, will give him a stone?
4: Or if he asks for fish will give him a serpent? (Matthew 7:9-10).

N: Every man, woman and child has the inalienable right to be free from hunger.

All: Share your bread with the hungry (Isaiah 58:7).

N: We must produce enough food for every human being on earth—and we can!

All: Share your bread with the hungry.

N: We must realize that all nations are interdependent and use our resources for mutual benefit—and we can!

All: Share your bread with the hungry.

N: Thus says the Lord:

1: Blessed are you that hunger now, for you shall be satisfied. Woe to you that are full now, for you shall hunger (Luke 6:21,25).

2: The Lord fills the hungry with good things and sends the rich away empty (Luke 1:53).

N: Thus says the Lord:

1: Behold, my servants shall eat, but you shall be hungry; behold, my servants shall drink, but you shall be thirsty; behold, my servants shall rejoice, but you shall be put to shame. For behold, I create new heavens and a new earth; and the former things shall not be remembered (Isaiah 65:13,17).

N: Thus says the Lord:

1: "Come, you that are blessed by my Father! Come and possess the kingdom which has been prepared for you ever since the creation of the world. I was hungry and you fed me, thirsty and you gave me a drink; I was a stranger and you received me in your homes, naked and you clothed me; I was sick and you took care of me, in prison and you visited me."

N: The righteous will then answer him:

2: "When, Lord, did we ever see you hungry and feed you, or thirsty and give you drink? When did we see you a stranger and welcome you in our homes, or naked and clothe you? When did we see you sick or in prison, and visit you?"

N: The King will reply:

1: "I tell you, whenever you did this for one of the least important of these brothers (and sisters) of mine, you did it for me!" (Matthew 25:34;41)

N: Thus says the Lord:

1: Give, and it will be given to you; good measure, pressed down, shaken together, running over, will be put into your lap. For the measure you give will be the measure you get back (Luke 6:38).

Session 6: Preparation for Christmas

This is the final session before a Christmas recess.

Getting Started: Sharing Christmas Memories

Ask the participants to share Christmas memories that focus upon the following:

1. Your most memorable Christmas. Why?
2. The most memorable Christmas gift you've received. Why?

Group Exercise: Bible Study of Anna

Distribute the Bible study handout on p. 106. Allow time for individual response and then total-group interaction.

Group Exercise: Letter to Self

As a way of retaining and carrying over some of the learnings from the fall until the group gathers again in January, ask the participants to write a letter to themselves. Give a piece of paper and a stamped envelope to each participant. After the session, collect these and then mail them two weeks prior to the starting date for the groups.

The letter to themselves can take any direction, but here are some suggested beginning points:

1. What have I learned from this group?
2. What do I hope to give and receive this Christmas season?
3. Is there some new way in which I hope to recognize Christ this Christmas?

Group Exercise: Affirmations

Distribute a blank sheet of colored paper and ask each participant to write her or his name across the top. These sheets will be passed around the circle and each group member will be invited to write an affirmation of the person whose name appears at the top of the sheet. After the exercise, the person to the left of each participant will read aloud that person's sheet of affirmations. After all have been read, then these sheets are to be included in the envelopes with members' letters to themselves.

It is the responsibility of the leaders to collect and mail these letters at the appropriate time.

Closing Exercise: Covenant and Prayer

This is a good opportunity to reevaluate the group's covenant and to

Bible Study

1. *Read Luke 2:36-38.*

   This Scripture tells of the prophetess Anna, an old woman who spent all of her time in the temple and who recognized the child Jesus as the Christ.

2. *Record your responses to the following questions:*

   a. Anna did two things when she saw the child Jesus. What were they?

   b. What do you think would have been your response?

   c. Do you really believe Anna knew who this child was and what he was to become? How do you think she knew?

   d. Have there been times and places in your life in which you have recognized Christ? Describe these. What was your response?

   e. Is there something you could do in your life now that would help you prepare for the coming of the Christ Child this Christmas? How do you think you would recognize him?

decide if there is any special way in which the group wishes to keep in touch after the recess, perhaps by having prayer partners, a social gathering, a time during each day or week when participants pause for prayer, and so on. A group decision should be reached.

The closing season of prayer can be concluded with the singing of a Christmas carol.

Session 7: First in the Two-Houses Triad

Getting Started: Dream of the Year

Ask participants to respond to this situation: "If there were no limitations, what would you want to accomplish or be able to experience in this new year?"

Group Exercise: Parable Creating

In this first session of a new triad, ask the participants to create a modern-day parable (it can be just a short sentence, an analogy, or a brief story) that completes this sentence: "Everyone who comes to me and hears what I say and acts upon it is like a. . . . "

The leader might offer an example, such as, " . . . is like a window, which, instead of being nailed shut, is free to open and close as it was created and intended to do."

Create and share the parables without identifying the scriptural text for the participants. They will be able to respond more creatively if they do not look up the text first.

Discipleship Exercise: "My Story and the Bible's Story"

Distribute this handout. Allow time for personal response, and for sharing.

(Follow instructions from previous "My Story" handout, page 87.)

Closing Exercise

This is probably a good time for participants to share with one another their experiences over the recess. It would also be good to share the responses of the participants as they received the letter in the mail from the last session.

A season of prayer can close this session.

(Page 1)

(PLEASE DO NOT TURN THE PAGE UNTIL COMPLETING THESE QUESTIONS.)

My Story and the Bible's Story

(Answer these questions as honestly as you can. Only you will be seeing your responses. You will need to keep this paper in your personal journal.)

1. Whom or what do you obey?

2. When are you most apt to get sloppy, or hasty, or careless?

3. Which image most symbolizes your life now: shifting sand or solid rock? Why?

4. Over this past year, or currently, are any "storms" brewing in your life? Can you identify any source of stress? Can you identify any ways you feel or have felt overwhelmed?

5. Rate the following (1-18) in terms of their importance to you as sources of strength (anchors) in your life:

___ Your parents (living or dead)
___ childhood memories and values
___ your small discussion group
___ close friends
___ personal achievements
___ prayer life
___ financial security
___ job security
___ the laws, police, courts, social order
___ values espoused by our church
___ the Bible
___ your family (spouse, children, and so on)
___ good health
___ the ways you are gifted
___ the return or presence of Christ
___ achievements of science and technology
___ our nation's military defense
___ (other) _____

6. I would rate my ability to listen (1 being superior; 5 being poor):

   1   2   3   4   5

   Why?

(Page 2)

A STORY FROM THE BIBLE

Read Luke 6:47-49. (You may also choose to read the same story in Matthew 7:24-27.)

How deeply is your faith rooted?

COME

LISTEN

ACT

(Page 3)

SYNTHESIS

1. Can you see connections or links between your personal story on page 1 and the biblical story on page 2? How do these two stories interact with each other?

2. God's Word can often break into our lives in unexpected and surprising ways. Are there any surprises from God's Word in this exercise?

3. Everyone is a builder. We build friendships, homes, marriages, ability to parent, careers, skills, talents, hopes, values, faith. What have you built in which you have devoted a significant amount of time and energy?

4. Our discipleship to Christ must be built, according to Jesus. It can be built to withstand the stresses and to overcome the obstacles that we inevitably encounter. Or it can be built with much less care.

   Jesus says that true disciples come to him, listen and then obey. For us to "come to Christ" means to come in prayer. We need to come to Christ in prayer in order to listen—to listen, in an attitude of prayer, to the words of Scripture—to listen to the voice of Christ speaking to us. And then we must obey by acting accordingly.

   This is, therefore, Jesus' rhythm for disciples:
   - to come in prayer
   - to listen to his words
   - to act accordingly.

   IS THIS RHYTHM WORKING IN YOUR LIFE?

(Page 4)

PRAYER AND PERSONAL DISCIPLINE

Over the next two weeks, repeat this prayer as often as is meaningful:

"Lord, teach me to come to you in prayer, to listen and to heed your voice. Amen."

Or feel free to write your own short prayer for daily use:

FOR YOUR REFLECTION

Christ lived, and in so living, devoted himself to building the kingdom of God on earth. Christ died, and in so dying, expressed the radical meaning of the kingdom translated into human reality. Christ was resurrected, and in his resurrection, enables others to join in the continuing task of building God's kingdom on earth. We are invited to be builders. The question is, will we?

Session 8: Second in the Two-Houses Triad

Getting Started: Wallet Exercise

Ask participants to look in their wallets or pocketbooks to find items that symbolize the following:

- something very precious to them
- something that troubles or concerns them
- something to which they devote a great amount of energy or time

These are to be shared with the total group.

Discipleship Exercise: Guided Meditation

Use the following guided meditation with the group. Remember, good leaders speak slowly, quietly, and take their time as they guide a group in meditation. Allow frequent times of silence.

Guided meditation—Text: Luke 6:47-49

Sit up in a relaxed position. . . . Breathe deeply. . . .

As the Spirit breathes into you . . . allow the leadership of your imagination to take you to another time and place . . . different from our own . . . to the time of Jesus . . . to his place. The Spirit, breathed within you, is a trustworthy guide as you allow your thoughts and feelings to follow and respond freely.

You find yourself walking along a lonely narrow path. The path you are taking is unfamiliar . . . you realize that you have never been here before. The sites are new sites.

For some reason, you have asked to meet Jesus. It was a daring thing for you. You had to muster up quite a bit of courage. . . . You could have seen him in a crowd; you could have listened to him preach in public; you could have witnessed one of his healings.

But you wanted more . . . a private time with him. The visit was arranged while Jesus was visiting nearby. He is alone now, praying, thinking. His disciples say that lately he has needed a lot of time to himself but that he will not mind the interruption. As you approach, you walk along a narrow path that leads down to a small, winding river. Jesus is sitting along the bank. You stand and look at him for some time a short distance away.

He sits motionless, in thought. He appears to you like a . . . like a carpenter. His large hands show the signs of rugged toil and labor . . . the hands of a carpenter.

You walk closer and sit down near him, facing the river as he does, watching as it quietly flows in front of you. Across the river are houses and people in the distance. But on this side of the river, you seem to be alone. Jesus is in a reflective mood.

"You've come to see me. You wanted to see me alone?" he asks. You respond affirmatively, nervously. "Don't be afraid," he smiles at you. He continues, "I am but a carpenter." Funny, you think to yourself, but that is just what was in your thoughts. "My father taught me how to build with my hands, how to conceive in my mind a piece of furniture to be built . . . a chair, a bed, a table . . . and to create it with my hands. I learned the craft as a child. I was raised to be a carpenter." Jesus stops and looks at you. Your eyes meet for the first time. "Did you come to ask something of me?" he inquires.

You respond that you just came to be with him, near him, to listen. He stares at you a long time, almost as if disbelieving. It was as if no one ever came to Jesus just to listen, but to get something, to take something away. You think how hard it must be to be in such demand . . . to have people follow you, crowd about you. No wonder he needs time alone.

Jesus calls you by your name. "A true disciple," he says, "is one who comes to me as you have come, who listens to my words, and who acts accordingly. Many come, but they do not come to listen. Some listen; few obey. A true disciple is like a good carpenter. Do you see those houses across the river?" He points to one house that is on higher ground. "Who built that house was a wise carpenter, for he built the foundation anchored deep into the rock. And when the rain comes down, the flood rises, and the gales blow and hurl themselves against that house, it will not fall." Jesus points to another house, lower than the first, "A foolish man built that house. Those who come to me and listen to my words but do not obey are like this man, for he has built his house on top of sand. And when the rains come down, the flood rises, and the gales blow and hurl themselves against this house, it will fall and be destroyed."

"My friend, you have come to me, you say, to listen. Well, now you have heard me. You have heard what you needed to hear; you have heard enough. Now I must leave you here, as you found me here . . . it is a place to think, to pray. But as I leave, I ask you, is your life anchored to the rock or built sitting upon the sand?" Jesus gets up in silence and leaves you with a kiss of peace. You watch him walk away into the distance.

You rehearse his words in your mind . . . "You have heard what you needed to hear," he said, "You have heard enough."

There is strength to your life. You know that. But there is weakness, too. There are shallow places, built upon sand, able to collapse. Perhaps Jesus was right. . . . Perhaps the foundation of your life is not set upon those things that hold . . . eternal things that will not vanish when the gales come and hurl themselves against you. You do need to sit in this place . . . to think where you found Jesus thinking. You can take these moments to do that. . . .

And when you are finished, you, too, can get up, in silence, look again across the river at the two houses Jesus used as a parable, and again walk down the narrow path that led you here . . . a path that now seems much more familiar, more comforting. Walk until you find yourself back in this group, among friends, and then open your eyes and rejoin us in this place.

After the guided meditation, urge the participants to record their responses in their personal journals. Then urge them to share their responses with the group as they feel comfortable.

Closing Exercise: Affirmation Circle

This is a good opportunity to repeat the affirmation circle from Session 2 as a closing exercise.

Session 9: Third in the Two-Houses Triad

Getting Started

Since the focus of this triad has been upon homes and foundations, it would be good to have participants share something from the beginning years of their lives in their childhood. Ask them to identify the center of warmth in their home. First, they could identify what kind of heat was used in their home and any experiences related to this. Then, which room was the warmest and who or what made this part of their house have a "warm feel" about it.

Discipleship Exercise: The Death-and-Resurrection Paradigm

Distribute the handout (p. 116). Urge participants to use their journals and information gained from the previous two sessions, plus their response to the sermon related to this Scripture and any other thoughts they have had, to respond to the questions on the handout.

When they have finished responding to the questions, ask participants to share their responses to the death-and-resurrection paradigm with a partner and then with the total group.

Closing Exercise: Communion with All Groups

This is the first opportunity for all the discipleship groups to gather in one group for an experience together. This session will conclude with Communion, with all members of the groups sitting in a large circle. An introduction can be given, a hymn sung, and a prayer offered. Then ask each small group to go to the table in silence to receive from one another the bread and the cup. A guided prayer and period of silence can conclude the session.

Session 10: First in the Gethsemane Triad

Getting Started: Values Continuum

Put out on the floor, a few feet apart, seven squares of paper marked as follows:

1	2	3	4	5	0	-1
					don't know	don't care

Ask people to get up and stand on or around the number that best represents their feelings or attitudes toward the following, in turn (stand on 1 if they feel very strongly, on 2 if less strongly, and so forth):

1. Your past week (weekend) (# 1, a good weekend; # 5, a bad weekend).
2. A position on a current controversial issue. Ask them, as a total group, to reflect on the following questions after they get in position.
   - Were you influenced by where others stood? Why or why not?
   - Was this awkward to have to declare yourself? Why?
   - How does it feel, standing there, declaring your values or beliefs?
3. Another current issue. Dialogue with a person who does not share your position. Attempt to understand each other . . . not convince!

After all are seated, talk about whether you did understand each other, and show difference between respect and tolerance.

Distribute the handout "Respect/Tolerance" to further the discussion.

Death and Resurrection

REVELATION
(from an encounter with the
Holy Spirit; a result of
listening, seeking, and waiting)

COMING ALIVE

From this death, how is Christ
calling you to New Life?

INSIGHT
(from your group and
personal experience over
the past several weeks)

DYING

In what way is Christ calling you
to die? to surrender? to let go?

"Here stands Christ, in the centre, between the old existence and the new, between me and myself." —Bonhoeffer

DEATH AND NEW LIFE

As spring arises from winter, so do we grow as disciples. Jesus said, "Unless a wheat grain falls on the ground and dies, it remains only a single grain; but if it dies, it yields a rich harvest" (John 12:24, *The Jerusalem Bible*).

HOW DOES THE DEATH AND NEW LIFE YOU HAVE DE-
SCRIBED ON THIS PAGE APPLY TO YOUR DAILY LIFE? WILL
IT HAVE AN IMPACT· ON THE WAY YOU LIVE OUT YOUR
DISCIPLESHIP IN THE WORLD?

Handout

Respect/Tolerance

RESPECT	TOLERANCE
It's active.	It's passive
It surrounds another person with appreciation.	I tend to "put up with" another person.
It requires in-depth insight into others.	It requires only passing knowledge of the other person.
It pulls others into my circle of concern.	It allows for detachment from others.
It does not require that we agree.	It does not require that we agree.

The First Baptist Church covenant . . .

"To respect the diversity of belief among ourselves as together we mature in Christian faith."

Discipleship Exercise: "My Story and the Bible's Story"

Distribute this handout. Allow time for personal response and for sharing. Urge participants to keep this handout in their personal journal. *(Follow instructions for previous "My Story" handouts.)*

Closing Exercise: To Follow the Leading of God's Spirit This Next Week

> But you are not carnal but spiritual if the Spirit of God *finds a home within you*. You cannot, indeed, be a Christian at all unless you have something of his Spirit in you. Now if Christ does live within you his presence means that your sinful nature is dead, but your spirit becomes alive because of the righteousness he brings with him. I said that our nature is 'dead' in the presence of Christ, and so it is, because of its sin. Once the Spirit of him who raised Christ Jesus from the dead lives within you he will, by the same Spirit, bring to your whole being . . . new strength and vitality. . . .
>
> So then, . . . you can see that we owe no duty to our sensual nature, or to live life on the level of the instincts. Indeed that way of living leads to certain spiritual death. But if on the other hand you cut the nerve of your instinctive actions by obeying the Spirit, you will live.
>
> —Romans 8:9-13 (Phillips, emphasis added)
>
> Everyone moved by the Spirit is a child of God.
>
> —Romans 8:14 (paraphrase)

List here four of the major ingredients in your coming week. Include those that will take extra preparation, those about which you feel uneasy or insecure, and those most in need of the Spirit's leading.

1.

2.

3.

4.

As you feel comfortable with your group, share two ways in your coming week in which you would most desire to be "moved by the Spirit." Paul says, " . . . if the Spirit of Christ does find a home within you, you are on your way to real living. Don't just live by instinct, or by your senses, live by following the leadership of the Spirit."

Pray for one another . . . for the leadership of the Spirit.

Handout

(Page 1)

(PLEASE DO NOT TURN THE PAGE UNTIL COMPLETING THESE QUESTIONS.)

My Story and the Bible's Story

(Answer these questions as honestly as possible. Only you will be seeing your responses. Keep this paper in your personal journal.)

1. How do you view sleep?   (Answer true or false.)
   _____ Sleep is a necessary interruption to my busy schedule.
   _____ Sleep is a time for me to be refreshed.
   _____ Sleep is a break from the confusion of life.
   _____ I often sleep to avoid a troubling situation.
   _____ Sleep is a time to allow my subconscious to take control.
   _____ I am tempted to sleep too much.
   _____ When there's nothing to do but sit and wait for someone, I find it difficult to stay awake.
   _____ It is frequently difficult for me to fall asleep.

2. The body, mind, soul, emotion and will—they all come together in making us whole persons. Sometimes we are not whole because our bodies can't/won't do all we desire to do. "The spirit is willing, but the flesh is weak" (Matthew 26:41b). Can you recall a time when you felt like this? How did you feel?

3. Are you likely to undertake a project when the risk of failure or disappointment is present? Why? Why not?

4. How do you deal with failure?
   ___ offer excuses or deny it   ___ avoid or ignore the situation
   ___ act as if you don't care   ___ accept it matter-of-factly
   ___ resign, quit, or give up   ___ take instant action to correct
   ___ feel guilt, self-pity, blame   ___ other_____

5. My ability to confront others, in love, when we have had a disagreement or problem is . . . (1 is strong; 7, weak)

   1   2   3   4   5   6   7

6. Think about recent disappointments in your life. When have you been disappointed by another person? Why?

   On what recent occasion do you believe you have disappointed others/another? Why?

(Page 2)

A STORY FROM THE BIBLE

Read Matthew 26:36-46. (You may also choose to read verses 31-35.)

As you read this Scripture, recall what the disciples had just experienced: their last week with Jesus, the week of his triumphal entry into Jerusalem, his attack on the money-changers in the temple, his conflict with the Pharisees, the crowds who were turning against him. Their emotions and spirits had been pushed, pulled, exhilarated, crushed. And now, they were afraid of the reality facing them.

(Page 3)

SYNTHESIS

1. Can you see connections or bridges between your personal story on page 1 and the biblical story on page 2? How do these stories interact with each other?

2. God's Word can often break into our lives in unexpected and surprising ways. Are there any surprises from God's Word in this exercise?

3. In this passage Christ is urging the disciples to be ready, prepared, alert, and yet . . .

   Life comes at us continuously . . . 60 seconds to every minute, 60 minutes to every hour, 24 hours to every day. Even when we sleep, life keeps coming. To think we could be prepared for every situation, every responsibility, every relationship we encounter in an average day, is the ultimate act of arrogance. Yet nothing so plagues the human soul as feeling unprepared for something.
   How do you respond to this?

4. At the end of their resources from the worry and fear of the final week in Jesus' life, the disciples opted for sleep. It has been said, "Faith begins when we reach the end of our resources." How do you feel at the end of your resources? Frustrated? Angry? Helpless? Embarrassed? . . . or Faithful?

5. As a disciple of Christ, are you, right now, alert? waiting? ready?

   For what are you waiting?
   For what are you ready?
   Is it possible to identify this?

6. Is your discipleship one of joy only? Or, as Christ asked the first disciples, are you ready to follow him into sacrifice, pain, disappointment, or fear?

(Page 4)

PRAYER AND PERSONAL DISCIPLINE

Over the next seven days, repeat this prayer as often is meaningful:

"At the limits of our resources, help us to place our trust in you, Lord. Amen."

Or feel free to write your own short prayer.

FOR YOUR REFLECTION

The issue is trust, plain and simple.
It is the issue of life and death.
It is certainly the issue of faith.
When we are weary, fearful, worn, overwhelmed, at the end of our limits, do we trust the Lord?

Or do we try to sleep away, work away, laugh away, shrug away, explain away our inability to cope.

Those first disciples could not bear to face the consequences of Jesus' action, could not bear to face the agony and fear which Jesus expressed in his prayer on that dark night in Gethsemane, could not bear to follow their Savior into crucifixion.

They did not trust. They slept.

Jesus, nearing the end of his limits and afraid of his own death, confronted it honestly in prayer. And from this encounter, he discovered the resources to say to God, "Not what I want, but what you want."

Session 11: Second in the Gethsemane Triad

Getting Started: Potluck Fellowship Meal

All small groups are invited to come together for a potluck meal to enjoy the fellowship around tables of food. Special events (like birthdays) of the participants can be celebrated at this time.

Discipleship Exercise: Guided Meditation

Urge participants to sit up, be comfortable, take things out of their laps and hands . . . to sit still . . . to allow their imagination to be a trustworthy guide for the next several minutes . . . to be conscious only of themselves and your voice. Then use the following meditation.

Guided meditation—Text: Matthew 26:31-46

It has been a week full of things to do and much remaining to be done. You return home on a Friday evening; it will be an evening to yourself. You kick off your shoes and sigh at the pleasant thought of a chance to relax. This is time to do what you want, not what others expect.

Are you aware of the sorts of things that typically wear you down? Are you aware of who or what it is that captures your energy and strength? . . . the things that worry you? . . . that create stress and anxiety?

Try to relax. Try to set aside these things that push and pull at you. Can you begin to relax your tired and weary body? Begin with your toes. Squeeze your toes together as tightly as you can. Feel the tension. Now, slowly allow your toes to relax. Feel the comfort in your toes. Let them really relax.

Now tense up the bottoms of your feet. You've been on your feet all day long, all week long. . . . Feel the tension in your feet. And now relax your feet. Feel the ease.

Move up your body. Tighten your thighs . . . as tightly as you can. And now relax your thighs. Then tighten your waist and chest and shoulders. And now relax.

Tighten up your face. Feel the tension in your mouth, forehead, around your eyes. Squeeze the muscles of your face tightly. And then relax them. Feel the tension as it leaves.

Finally, your hands. Make them into a tight fist. Feel the pressure, the squeeze. And then relax, every finger, joint, the palm of your hand . . . relaxed.

Feel your whole body now, relaxed. Every point of contact with the chair, the floor, relaxed, comfortable. This is the ease you have been seeking all day. Just rest. You deserve this time, and you know it. . . .

With your eyes still closed, you gaze out to encounter the face of Christ before you. What does this face look like? Is it white, or brown, or tan, or red? Is it male or female? Is Christ a person of modern times, or ancient, or is he timeless? Does the face look familiar? As you gaze at this face of love, what stands out? The eyes? The mouth? A certain expression?

Christ is here, right here with you, to ask you to do something. What you are being asked to do may be pleasing to God, but it is certainly an interruption to your peace and quiet.

What is it that Christ is asking you to do? Could it be something in your life, or from your past week? Is it a bad habit to break? A floundering relationship with a friend or colleague? An injustice to address? Does Christ want you to reach out to a person in need? to take a personal risk? to trust more? to pray more . . . ?

Whatever it is, the request could not have come at a worse time. You really are worn and weary. Can't it wait? Perhaps you offer an excuse to Christ. You're just not up to undertaking anything quite like this tonight. You couldn't do it justice now. Maybe tomorrow.

Or it could be that whatever Christ is asking you to do you feel unprepared for . . . inadequate for the task . . . maybe even unwilling because the cost or risk is simply too great? In some way, for some reason, you feel lacking.

The face of Christ is still before you. And you find yourself trying to look down, look away, avoid the gaze of Christ. You want to get away, hide.

After a time, you hear Christ quietly sigh, pause, then turn away, and leave. How do you feel? How do you deal with this? How do you respond to the disappointment of Christ? Do you feel pain? bewilderment? defensiveness? guilt? sadness? anger at yourself? at the situation? Sit there and feel this moment. . . .

Finally, one more image comes to your mind. It is a scene from the life of Christ. . . . in the garden of Gethsemane one evening. You see Christ again, with several of the beloved disciples. You see how quiet the disciples appear. How weary they look! And again, you see the disappointment of Christ, for the disciples could not stay awake to wait with Christ, to pray, to keep watch.

And you think how often disciples disappoint Christ. You have

disappointed Christ . . . tonight . . . often . . . so have all disciples.
You feel, for as long as you need, the pain this causes *(long pause)*.

And in your own time, you take leave of this biblical scene, and then bring yourself back once again, here with our group.

Ask participants to journalize after the meditation is completed. Then they can share with each other the insights they have gained.

Closing Exercise: Jesus and Accountability

Read the scriptural selection after distributing the following handout. Use the questions as a basis for discussion and group evaluation. Close by inviting prayers for your small group.

Handout

SUGGESTED GROUP CLOSING

[Jesus] came to the disciples and found them asleep; and he said to Peter, 'What! Could none of you stay awake with me one hour? Stay awake, and pray that you may be spared the test. The spirit is willing, but the flesh is weak.'

He went away a second time to pray. . . . He came again and found them asleep, for their eyes were heavy. So he left them and went away again; and he prayed the third time, using the same words as before.

Then he came to the disciples and said to them, 'Still sleeping? Still take your ease? The hour has come! The Son of Man is betrayed to sinful men' (Matthew 26:40-46, NEB).

Jesus confronts his disciples with his own disappointment at their failure to support him. It is clear that Jesus loves them enough to hold them accountable for their actions.

All discipling communities must love one another enough to hold each other accountable. This midpoint affords all of us in the group a good opportunity to evaluate how we hold one another accountable:

What does it mean to be accountable to one another in this group?

Are we honest enough to confront, in love?

Are we helpful to one another?

Do we share our disappointments? our own failures? our hopes for other group members?

Close by inviting prayers for your group, for the role it has and will play in helping you grow in discipleship to Christ.

Session 12: Third in the Gethsemane Triad

Getting Started: Update

Use the brief question "How is it with you today?" to focus upon one another.

Group Exercise: Further Questions and Insights from the Biblical Text

If leaders feel there is plenty of time in this session, then participants could work in pairs on each of the questions on the "Further Questions and Insights from the Biblical Text." If leaders feel that time is limited, then participants could work in pairs or triads, with one or two questions assigned to each group. In addition, every group could be assigned the first question.

After a time of work on the Scripture, have a time of sharing answers and responses. Only to the first question is there a definite "right" answer.

Discipleship Exercise: The Death-and-Resurrection Paradigm

Distribute the handout "Growing into the Full Stature of Christ," urging participants to use their journals and the information gained from the previous two sessions, as well as any response to the sermon that was related to this Scripture and any other thoughts they have had from their discipline of prayer and spiritual reflection.

Allow time for each person to complete the sheet.

After participants have had a time of individual work, encourage them to share what they have learned and any decisions they have made.

Closing Exercise: Walking Through the Death and Resurrection of Our Lord

As this session will probably be held near the time of Palm Sunday and Holy Week, point out that your purpose is to rehearse the steps taken by Jesus during his final week of conflict and victory.

Ask the group to "walk" together through the events of this week. Invite participants to stand in one end of the room. Place a card on the floor by the group, labeled "Palm Sunday." As the group stands at this place, ask them to respond to these questions:

"If we were at the first Palm Sunday, what would we be hearing?"

"What would we be feeling at this point?"

After a period of sharing, ask the group to take one step forward.

Place another card on the floor by them and ask for responses to the same questions. Have the group continue through the Holy Week experiences, using cards with the following labels:

Palm Sunday
Jesus' Confrontation with Money-Changers in the Temple
The Last Supper
Prayer in Gethsemane
Jesus' Arrest
The Trials before Pilate and Herod
The Crucifixion
The Empty Tomb and Resurrection Appearances

Close with a prayer that we have the discipline and courage to retrace these steps as we move through this coming week.

Further Questions and Insights from the Biblical Text

In our small discipleship group, we have explored in these most recent sessions the story of Jesus and his disciples in Gethsemane. We began by comparing our own personal life story and the story from the Bible. We entered the passage with our imaginations in a guided meditation. We imagined our own failure to do what Jesus asks. Now, this week we will attempt to hear what Christ is calling us to do with our lives in the light of his text.

Here are more questions and issues for your reflection.

1. For the fun of it, what do you think the word "Gethsemane" means?

    a. a place of beauty
    b. garden of prayer
    c. the name of the family who owned the garden
    d. a grove of olive trees
    e. an oil press

2. One of the most interesting aspects of the stories of Jesus' life is that they are told by four different authors, each with his own perspective.

    Compare Mark 14:32-42 with Luke 22:39-46.
    What are the differences between the two stories?
    Which version do you prefer? Why?
    (The story is also told in Matthew 26:36-46 and John 18:2.)

3. Why do you believe that Jesus asked his disciples to "watch and pray"?

    a. He was truly nervous about his arrest, about being discovered.
    b. He wanted to be alone; he wanted no one to invade his privacy.
    c. He wanted close friends to be near him.
    d. He wanted his disciples to pray for him because he felt weak and afraid.

    e. _____

4. There are interesting parallels in the Scripture:

> Jesus' three times of prayer
> His three returns to the three disciples
> Peter's three denials
> Three hours of agony on a cross (three crosses)
> Three days in the tomb

Is this just coincidence?

5. In Mark 14:38, Jesus says, "The spirit indeed is willing, but the flesh is weak." What is he saying here to the disciples? What does this verse mean?

SHARE YOUR RESPONSES WITH OTHERS. Only to #1 is there a definite "right" answer.

Growing into the Full Stature of Christ

> *By baptism we were buried with Christ Jesus, and lay dead, in order that, as Christ was raised from the dead . . . so also we might set our feet upon the new path of life.*
>
> *For if we become one with Christ in death, we shall also be one with him in resurrection. We know that the person we once were has been crucified with Christ, for the destruction of the sinful self. . . . If we thus died with Christ, we believe that we shall also come to life with him* (Romans 6:4-7, *NEB, adapted*).

A. Read your journal entries from the past two sessions and read the related scriptural passage. In the following steps, you will examine these resources in the light of a "death-resurrection" model for discipleship growth.

   MAKE YOUR RESPONSES AS SPECIFIC AS POSSIBLE!

B. **Becoming One with Christ in Death**

   DYING TO THE SINFUL SELF . . .

   From the scriptural passage and your journal responses, can you understand to what God is calling you to die (to surrender, to let go, to turn away from, to release)?

   Are there obstacles that prevent you from realizing the full stature of Christ?

C. **FOR YOUR REFLECTION**
   "Here stands Christ, in the centre, between me and myself, between the old existence and the new."—(Bonhoeffer)

   Your hearts and minds must be made completely new, and you must put on the new self, which is created in God's likeness . . . (Ephesians 4:23, *TEV*).

Handout

D. **Becoming One with Christ in Resurrection**

PUTTING ON THE NEW SELF . . .   COMING TO NEW
LIFE IN CHRIST . . .

From out of this death, you are being called by God into new life.

What is the specific promise of "resurrection" that God is holding
for you?

E. **Application to Daily Discipleship**

Reflect upon this "death and resurrection" in your life. What
difference will it make in your daily ministry with others?

Will it change how you act as a disciple for Christ? in what ways?

F. As you feel comfortable, share with others in your group. Dedicate,
affirm, support.

Session 13: First in the Bethany-Home Triad

Getting Started: Introduce the "New"

Ask participants to pair off and share with their partner two things about themselves or their lives which no one else in the group would be likely to know. Then ask the partners to introduce the "new" about the other person to the total group.

This is a good time to urge each group member to engage in a "ministry of interpretation" to the wider church and to their friends beyond the church. If they have not shared what has happened to them in this discipleship-group experience, now is a good time to begin this witness to their growth toward Christ. The pledge to confidentiality was not to share beyond the group what others have spoken within the group. Participants can feel free, however, to share their own learnings and insights beyond the group.

Discipleship Exercise: "My Story and the Bible's Story"

Distribute the handout "My Story and the Bible's Story." Allow participants time to fill it out and then to share with the group. *(Follow instructions for previous "My Story" handouts.)*

Closing Exercise: May God Grant You Strength

Use the closing exercise from Session 3.

Urge participants to bring to the next session a sign or symbol of spring, which they will give to another participant as a gift.

Session 14: Second in the Bethany-Home Triad

Getting Started

Each person should have brought to this session a symbol of spring and new life. Begin the session by inviting a response to this question: "Have you had meaningful experiences this spring, enjoying and appreciating the created world?"

Then ask one person at a time to share his or her symbol of spring with one other person, stating why this symbol is important. Then the person receiving the gift will share his or her gift with another, and so forth until all have shared and received.

Handout

(Page 1)

(PLEASE DO NOT TURN THE PAGE UNTIL COMPLETING THESE QUESTIONS.)

My Story and the Bible's Story

(Answer these questions as honestly as possible. Only you will be seeing your responses. Keep this paper in your personal journal.)

1. Nearly every family or group of friends uses dinners to celebrate important events. What can you recall celebrating around a dinner table?

2. When you are misunderstood, are you . . .
   __defensive? __hurt? __angry? __explosive? __persistent enough to keep on trying? __conciliatory? __apt to compromise quickly or adapt to others' expectations? __apt to ignore your own feelings or not express them? __(other) _____

3. Are you more likely to:
   • care about a global issue of social concern?
   • respond to a specific need of a person you know?

4. When faced with a choice of work or conversation, which would you more likely favor?

5. Identify several "small" ways that you serve or help others.

6. How do you react to the poor?
   Do they threaten you?_____ Do you pity them?_____ Do you blame the poor for their situation? Do you wish they'd "get their act together"?_____ Are you an active advocate for the poor?_____ Do you mistrust them?_____ Do you not think very much about the poor?_____ Do you identify with the poor?_____

7. Name one person you know personally whom you greatly respect. How do you show or express your respect for this person?

(Page 2)

A STORY FROM THE BIBLE

Read: John 12:1-8.

As you read this passage in the Bible, recall that Jesus had just resurrected Lazarus from the dead. Mary and Martha, Lazarus' two sisters, had called for Jesus the moment his health deteriorated. But Jesus tarried, and by the time he arrived, Lazarus had been dead for a while. The sisters openly confronted their friend Jesus with their anger.

This dinner follows Jesus' miracle of bringing Lazarus back to life. It is probable that nearly everyone at the dinner table was also present at the miracle.

Note particularly the actions of Mary and Martha.

Handout

(Page 3)

SYNTHESIS

1. Can you see connections or bridges between your personal story on page 1 and the biblical story on page 2? How do these stories interact?

2. God's Word can often break into our lives in unexpected and surprising ways. Are there any surprises from God's Word in this exercise?

3. The biblical account tells of two women who found ways to serve others. It is obvious that Martha had a deep commitment to her ministry: hers was a ministry of hosting others, of opening her home (she was probably the eldest of the three) to friends and guests, of preparing food and a loving environment for others to enjoy.

    Mary's ministry was her ability to listen, to engage in thoughtful dialogue, and her willingness to show respect for one she admired.

    Too often we think of ministry in very public yet narrow terms, such as preaching or pastoral care. Mary and Martha remind us by their actions that every follower of Christ has a ministry to perform.

    WHAT IS *YOUR* MINISTRY? If possible, draw a symbol of your ministry here. (If necessary, use words in describing it.)

4. How can your small discipleship group support, enhance and affirm you in your ministry?

Handout

(Page 4)

PRAYER AND PERSONAL DISCIPLINE

Over the next two weeks, until your group meets again, repeat this prayer as often as is meaningful:

> *"Help me, I pray, as I become a person who ministers in your name. Amen."*

FOR YOUR REFLECTION

> *"It is unmistakably clear that the term 'priest' as used in the New Testament does not refer to officiants in a church building, but describes all Christians in their role as the priesthood of all believers."*
>
> *Every Christian is called to a ministry that flows directly from the Gospel. Whoever has the Gospel has also a ministry. Every historian will recognize that this was the teaching of the Protestant reformers."*—Oscar E. Feucht, *Everyone a Minister* (Saint Louis: Concordia Publishing House, 1977), pp. 40 and 51.
>
> *Discipleship is not only a journey inward to discover our true selves and the call of Christ. It is also a journey outward, to serve, to share, to sacrifice. We must learn to journey in both directions.*

Discipleship Exercise: Guided Meditation

Lead the participants in the guided meditation that follows. Allow time for silence.

Guided Meditation—Text: John 12:1-8

Often we unconsciously carry emotional pressure in our bodies. We allow the worries and frets of our daily lives to fill our minds.

Often worry localizes in our heads; can you feel any tightness, any tension in your forehead? around your eyes? in the back of your head? Relax your mouth; feel the tension or worry leave your head. Push the worry down . . . down through your neck, your trunk, collecting all tension along the way as it moves down. Feel the empty space left behind.

Your legs and feet have been carrying you places all day long. They are likely to be tired. Push the worn out feeling, the tiredness, the worry, and the fret all out . . . through the bottom of your feet, until you are totally and completely relaxed.

Breathe in a deep breath. Fill your lungs. Hold it . . . and release. Push, push it out. Then breathe in again . . . and release.

Begin to fill the emptiness of your mind with an image of a dinner table . . . a dinner table in Bethany of Judea. Many people are there at the table with you. The time is several thousand years ago—yet you still feel at home. You belong. Many trays of food are scattered around the tables. . . . The food has been picked over . . . and you are full. You look across the room full of friendly faces. You notice Lazarus . . . Lazarus, who was dead only days before and whom Jesus raised to life. Lazarus, looking so alive, so grateful. Can you see the joy—the thanksgiving in Lazarus' face?

Over Lazarus' shoulder, you notice the door leading to the kitchen. Martha comes out to collect dishes and food. She seems to enjoy serving you and the others.

Finally your eyes rest upon Jesus, for there is now commotion near him. You cannot see what is going on, but you hear the murmuring of people nearby. You see people pulling back. In order to see, you stand and look over at Jesus' feet. Mary is there. She is leaning over Jesus and dramatically pouring burial ointment over his feet. Now she is drying his feet with her long, wavy black hair. Your first response is how strange Mary's actions appear to be. She seems to be preparing a living person for burial. But the more you watch her, the more you recognize what a beautiful thing she is doing . . .

what a beautiful way she is serving her Lord. And the scent of the ointment reaches you and envelops the entire room. Can you smell the beautiful, gentle fragrance?

Jesus has been watching Mary, lovingly; what is awkward to some others, is not to him. Clearly, he is moved, touched by her action.

But now he looks up, and he sees you standing there across the room. Your eyes meet. And in his glance he seems to be asking you a question. He looks at Mary again, then at you . . . and you know he must be wondering: This is how Mary serves me . . . how are you serving me? Are you content only to sit in the grandstand and watch . . . or will you get involved?

Mary finishes cleansing his feet. Jesus rises, and, with all of the people in the room, he beckons you to join him.

You walk toward Jesus . . . to a quiet part of the room, near a window. The two of you face the window; Jesus holds out his hand, saying, "Look out of this window as if it were an opening through the centuries framing your life today. You have seen Martha serve at this dinner. You have seen Mary serve at my feet. How do you see, through the opening of this window, your service to me? Do you see your own service in your own day—in your life? Do you serve through a newfound friend? through a cause or issue? through your family? through your vocation?"

Jesus is asking you to get a picture of the ways in which you feel called to serve him. . . . Serve him with all of your life . . . not just a part. . . . Serve him in daily ways . . . with your time, your creativity, your hopes and aspirations.

Take some time to look through this window, to look upon your life and, like Martha and Mary, to find new ways, old ways, natural ways, sacrificial ways in which you feel called to serve Jesus Christ *(long pause)*.

As you are ready to leave, you notice that Jesus has returned to the others. Deep in thought, you leave through the door and walk back across the years to this time, to this place. Whenever you are ready, rejoin us by opening your eyes.

It is now _____ P.M. You have until _____ P.M. to journalize. Write down or draw a picture of the image that came to you during this meditation.

It might be noted that the guided meditations in some sessions could be prerecorded on tape or done with all groups together in one place, such as in the church sanctuary.

After the meditation, respond to these questions: What in today's context would be service comparable to that given by Mary? by Martha? Were any new avenues of service opened as you looked through the window upon your life?

Closing Exercise

There is a need at this point for a verbal evaluation within each group, showing their response to the format and approach of these small discipleship groups. Some evaluation would be helpful here to inform future planning.

The closing can be a sharing of concerns and a season of prayer.

Session 15: Third of the Bethany-Home Triad

Getting Started: Update

Use the simple, "How is it with you, today?" exercise.

Discipleship Exercise: The Death-and-Resurrection Paradigm

Use the handout "My Accountability to the Biblical Text." Provide opportunity for individual work and group sharing.

Group Experience: Holy Communion

Leaders can ask one participant to bake the bread and someone to bring the juice.

Discussion/reflection for the bread:
> "In what ways have you shared the brokenness of your life
>   through this small group?"

Discussion/reflection for the cup:
> "In what ways have you felt nourished and refreshed
>   by this group?"

Closing Exercise: Total Group Closing

Have the total group gather for a hymn, litany of celebration, and closing circle, using the handout for the "Group Closing."

My Accountability to the Biblical Text

SCRIPTURAL TEXT: SERVING IN BETHANY (John 12)

One or two major insights from "My Story and the Bible's Story." Record them in this box:

One or two primary revelations from the guided meditation. Record them in this box:

From the insights you learned above, as well as thinking you have done about this text and its meaning for your life, answer the questions below as specifically as you can . . .

SPECIFICALLY

YIELDING . . . What is God inviting you to surrender? How are you being asked to yield to God's will or way?

CALLING . . . How is God calling you to serve? Toward what new level of discipleship is Christ calling *you?*

CLARIFYING

Final step: Share with a partner in your group. Allow this person to ask several questions of you that will help you clarify and verbalize the ways you need to yield to God and the ways you feel called by God.

John 12:1-8 and John 13

INSIGHTS

According to John, Mary was to choose the time and the place for her loving, prophetic act. And Mary chose the celebration of her brother Lazarus' resurrection from the dead.

It is important to note what was happening here, as described in the Gospel of John. Just before the dinner party, the Jewish leaders in Jerusalem had determined that Jesus must be killed (John 11:53). Jesus was wanted as a common criminal. Lazarus, too, was to be killed, "since it was on his account that many of the Jews were . . . believing in Jesus" (12:11).

Mary knew that death stalked at the door of this home. But Mary had learned, probably from the Pharisees when she was a child, to believe in the resurrection of the dead. She was not frightened at Jesus' impending death. Indeed she may have seen Lazarus' resurrection as a symbol of Jesus' resurrection. She alone understood.

And so it was that at this dinner party Mary went to the place where she had stored the precious perfume. Jesus caught her movement out of the corner of his eye. Seeing the nard in her hands, he knew that his time was drawing near. A foretaste of the fear he would experience later in Gethsemane was in the room. Jesus was to be prepared for burial before his death. His friend Mary would kneel at his feet, like a servant, and wash his feet with burial ointment.

1. In what ways does Mary's service seem to have been a risky thing to do?

2. Why do you suppose she did this despite the risks?

3. Have you ever felt called to do risky things in serving Christ?

Group Closing

Opening Hymn: "Go, Make of All Disciples" (Adkins)

A Litany of Celebration

Leader: We are a community of disciples.

People: We are a community of disciples.

Leader: We have shared in a yearlong journey together, seeking to know more fully what it means to be a disciple of Christ.

People: We are "disciples-in-the-making."

Leader: Our journey included words of Scripture. "He said to them, 'Throw your net out on the right side of the boat, and you will catch some.' So they threw the net out and could not pull it back in, because they had caught so many fish" (John 21:6-7, TEV).

People: As disciples of Christ we must learn to cast our nets in new waters. Lord, make us open to your suggestions.

Leader: "Why do you call me, 'Lord, Lord,' and yet don't do what I tell you? Anyone who comes to me and listens to my words and obeys them—I will show you what he is like. He is like a man who, in building his house, dug deep and laid the foundation on rock. The river flooded over and hit that house but could not shake it, because it was well built. But anyone who hears my words and does not obey them is like a man who built his house without laying a foundation; when the flood hit that house it fell at once—and what a terrible crash that was!" (Luke 6:46-49, TEV).

People: As disciples of Christ we must learn to come, to listen, to act. Lord, teach us to come to you in prayer, to listen and to heed your voice.

Leader: "Once more Jesus went away and prayed, 'My Father, if this cup of suffering cannot be taken away unless I drink it, your will be done.' He returned once more and found the disciples asleep; they could not keep their eyes open. Again Jesus left them, went away, and prayed the third time, saying the same words. Then he returned to the disciples and said,

'Are you still sleeping and resting?' Look! The hour has come for the Son of Man to be handed over to the power of sinful men. Get up, let us go. Look, here is the man who is betraying me!' '' (Matthew 26:42-46, TEV).

People: As disciples of Christ we must learn to trust. At the limits of our resources, help us to place our trust in you, Lord.

Leader: "Then Mary took a whole pint of very expensive perfume made of pure nard, poured it on Jesus' feet and wiped them with her hair. . . . One of Jesus' disciples, Judas Iscariot— the one who was going to betray him—said, 'Why wasn't this perfume sold for three hundred silver coins and the money given to the poor?' . . . But Jesus said, 'Leave her alone! Let her keep what she has for the day of my burial. You will always have poor people with you, but you will not always have me' '' (John 12:3-8).

People: As disciples of Christ we must learn to serve. Help us, we pray, as we become persons who minister in your name, O Lord.

Leader: Our journey included times of meditation.

People: You speak to us, O Lord, in the quiet, with a still, small voice. You speak to us through our imaginations as we are led to other times and places. You speak to us in many ways, and as disciples of Christ our task is to learn to listen.

Leader: On our discipleship journeys we learned the truth of dying and being resurrected. Jesus said, "I am telling you the truth: a grain of wheat remains no more than a single grain unless it is dropped into the ground and dies. If it does die, then it produces many grains" (John 12:24, TEV).

People: "For if we become one with Christ in death, we shall also be one with him in resurrection. We know that the person we once were has been crucified with Christ, for the destruction of the sinful self. . . . If we thus died with Christ, we believe that we shall also come to life with him" (Romans 6:5-8, NEB, adapted).

Leader: We are a community of disciples. Let us affirm one another.

People: As Christ affirms us.

Leader: Let us lift one another.

People: As Christ lifts us.

Leader: Let us accept one another.

People: As Christ accepts us.

Leader: We affirm you.

People: As Christ affirms us.

Leader: "Your hearts and minds must be made completely new, and you must put on the new self, which is created in God's likeness . . . " (Ephesians 4:23-24, TEV).

Unison: We are the community of disciples. We are the new creation. May we do all to the glory and honor of God. Amen.

Closing Circle

Blest be the tie that binds
Our hearts in Christian love;
The fellowship of kindred minds
Is like to that above. Amen.

Passing of the Peace
"May the love of Christ be with you . . . and with you."

Refreshments

Fellowship

Sign-up Scroll for Next Year's Groups

The Adult Discipleship Plan

(This resource was written by the Project Associates of the First Baptist Church of Dayton. It was adopted by the church executive council. The intent of the plan is to describe the ways in which adult discipleship is a priority in the church's planning processes.)

A Lifelong Journey

Christian discipleship is a lifelong pilgrimage—a journey that each follower of Jesus Christ is called to make. Because this is true, no adult can ever be said to have "arrived," any more than can a child or a young person. Always there is need for educational settings that provide opportunities for those "teachable moments" in which a disciple discovers anew the meaning of his or her discipleship—arenas that enrich the pilgrimage, challenge the journeyer, and confront the individual disciple at whatever stage of growth he or she is at any given time.

For example, a Christian disciple cannot be merely a parent; rather, he or she is called to be a Christian parent. A disciple cannot be merely an engineer or a teacher, a clerk typist or a janitor; rather, he or she is called to apply the full measure of Christian faith, as he or she understands it, to all of the situations confronted daily on the job. Interpersonal relationships also require the application of call and response, which is at the heart of discipleship.

Because adult disciples are never all at the same point of the journey, there is a need for a variety of settings or models that will encourage individual disciples to grow in meaningful response to their own calling to be disciples in all of the aspects of their lives. Some of these experiences facilitate journeys inward, which equip the disciples; others encourage journeys outward, which extend their ministry. Wherever possible, the model or setting should offer opportunities for both kinds of journey.

The Journey Begins

On his or her faith journey, a Christian may be able to point to one time that marked the beginning of that journey, but throughout life adults may feel the need to "begin again," and so all disciples—new, returning, and continuing—are included here.

Invitation

First-time converts, disciples wishing to transfer membership from other churches, and persons desiring formally to renew or reaffirm their commitment to Jesus Christ—all are invited to make that faith statement publicly by coming forward in response to the invitation at the close of the Sunday worship service. (Pastors) (This parenthetical note and those in the following sections indicate the person or persons responsible.)

New Creation Fellowship

This fellowship meets on the first Friday of each month, September through June, and is hosted by the pastors and their spouses to acquaint persons with our church and to help them become integrated into its life. Prospective members, new members, and members seeking to make a deeper step of commitment are encouraged to participate in six sessions that focus on (1) the theology of the Baptists and of First Baptist Church; (2) the history of our church; (3) information about American Baptist Churches, U.S.A.; (4) expectations of members through study of the church covenant and what members can expect of our church; (5) the structure of decision making for our church; and (6) the programs and ministry of our church. Each session provides opportunities for getting acquainted and sharing in Christian fellowship, studying one aspect of the nature of our church, prayer and devotion, and opportunities for involvement in the life of our church. (See the next section of this chapter.) (Congregational Care Committee, Board of Deacons; pastors)

Counseling

Counseling is available for returning and continuing disciples with pastors and/or selected deacons. For new disciples, a prebaptism session is held by the pastors. (Pastors; Congregational Care Committee, Board of Deacons)

Baptism

Participation in the ordinance of baptism is an act of discipleship. Families, faith partners, and the congregation are encouraged to celebrate with the new member this special time of Christian dedication. (Pastors; Baptism and Congregational Care Committees, Board of Deacons)

Faith Partners

Each person beginning the Christian journey should have a faith partner, a member of the congregation assigned by the Board of Deacons, who acts as friend, supporter and liaison between the individual and the wider church community. Faith partners are chosen shortly after a person makes known his or her desire to begin or renew discipleship, and involvement will continue for a period of six months. Faith partners are encouraged to participate in the activities planned for new members, such as a prebaptism session with the pastors and one *New Creation Fellowship* session. They also are encouraged to keep in touch on a one-to-one basis, helping the new member to feel at home and to become involved in the church, and being a source of support for spiritual growth. (Congregational Care Committee, Board of Deacons)

Right Hand of Fellowship

The *Right Hand of Fellowship* is extended at the time a disciple joins the church and is a symbol of that event. It follows (1) baptism, which is usually by immersion in the case of new converts; (2) the receipt of a letter of church membership for those moving their membership from another Christian denomination; or (3) acceptance on Christian experience for disciples wishing to restore their commitment. The Right Hand of Fellowship is a part of the first Communion service with these new members. Candidates for membership and the congregation repeat pledges of commitment to one another and read the church covenant as a reminder of their promises to God and to one another through the church. Each new member receives a copy of the church covenant at this time. The deacons honor new members at a luncheon following the service. (Pastors; Congregational Care Committee, Board of Deacons)

The Journey Together

Jesus said, "For where two or three are gathered in my name, there am I in the midst of them" (Matthew 18:20, RSV). The Christian journey is not made alone. The church provides numerous opportunities for Christian growth as we journey together.

Adult Church School Classes

The class setting provides opportunities to learn about the Bible and our faith and to apply the Christian faith to life situations. Such classes are a place of identity within the framework of the larger church and are an important source of fellowship. Such classes are encouraged to deal creatively with the question of discipleship and to empower their members to engage in specific actions of caring and serving ministry. (Adult Ministries Committee, Board of Christian Education)

Small Groups

Disciples, whether new, returning or continuing, often express a need for the more intimate setting of small groups that are organized for short or long time spans in order for members to explore faith, increase caring, and outreach.

1. *Yearlong Discipleship-Journey Groups.* Covenantal groups are organized to meet every other week, probably on Sunday evenings, for twelve to fifteen sessions, beginning in late September and concluding in early spring, with a recess during the Christmas season. Such groups explore biblical passages that reveal the nature and meaning of Christian discipleship. The sessions are designed to build connections between the personal stories of participants and the Bible story; to encourage participants to enter into the Bible story imaginatively and allow it to speak to them; to hold participants accountable to the biblical word and the Spirit's leading; to provide critical analysis and insight into the text; to build a supportive, trusting covenantal group which involves intimacy, accountability, and intercessory prayer; and to help participants understand and share their call to discipleship and ministry in the world. Co-leaders are selected by the planning committee and trained within a leaders' group. Participants are recruited each year prior to the launch of fall program. (Adult Ministries Committee, Board of Christian Education)

2. *Short-Term Discipleship Groups.* As needed or desired, small groups are organized, which center on a specific need, goal, or season of the church year. Possible models include:

a. *Lenten Journey Groups.* Neighborhood groups may be organized to meet weekly in homes during the Lenten season and will focus upon Christ's passion and its implications for our lives. (Congregational Care Committee, Board of Deacons)

b. *Bible Study Groups.* Small groups may be organized from time to time for the purpose of studying and understanding the Scriptures, either in neighborhood settings or at the church. (Adult Ministries Committee, Board of Christian Education)

c. *Support Groups.* From time to time, groups may be formed to support and meet the needs of specific groups of persons such as parents, singles, persons with a shared sense of vocation, and so on. (Congregational Care Committee, Board of Deacons; Adult Ministries

Committee, Board of Christian Education)

d. *Women's Circles*. American Baptist Women's Society members have traditionally met in "circle" groups each month for study, worship, mission-service outreach, and fellowship. (American Baptist Women's Society)

The Journey Inward

The journey inward that equips disciples for ministry often requires time apart from the "dailyness" of life and its responsibilities, time that permits disciples to grapple with faith development and to seek spiritual nourishment.

The Overnight Retreat

This model, an overnight retreat beginning with dinner on Friday evening and ending midafternoon on Saturday, has proven helpful for those who have participated. One or two overnight retreats are planned each program year to enable persons to broaden the base of faith from which they minister in the various contexts of their lives. Such retreats should offer variety in programming and in the kinds of persons for whom they are planned. For example: one retreat might attract adults of a variety of ages and backgrounds; another might be designed for married couples; another for singles; another for senior citizens; and so on. The retreat format includes such ingredients as Bible study, meditation, fun times, nature walks, exploration of talents and spiritual needs, and challenges for growth and ministry. (Congregational Care Committee, Board of Deacons; Family Life Chairperson, Board of Christian Education)

The Journey Outward

Groups in Ministry

Groups are formed for a period of time, dependent upon the duration of a specific project, to plan, fund, staff, and implement projects of ministry and/or personal evangelism to persons, groups or agencies beyond the church. For example: a refugee mission support group, a missioners mission support group, a "partners in urban mission" support group. (Boards of Christian Education, Mission, and Deacons)

Theologian in Residence

Biennially, a prominent theologian is invited to be in residence for a week in our church and the community to open dialogue between theologians and the laity and to make theology more accessible to persons in the community. This week of highlighting theological concepts and study has a central theme and may include such features as the Sunday morning sermon, church school talk-back with adults and youth, evening lectures, morning seminars, and presentations at United Theological Seminary. (Worship Committee, Board of Deacons)

Institute of Christian Growth

In alternate years, those years when we do not have a theologian in residence, we hold an Institute of Christian Growth which offers several classes designed to increase the understanding of the faith and its application to daily life. It shall be open to the wider community. Its curriculum shall include offerings in Bible study, theological study, and practical application of the gospel. (Worship Committee, Board of Deacons)

New Creation Fellowship

(Resources developed by Stephen Jones and Bruce Morgan)

One of the most critical problems facing the inclusive church is how it integrates new members into the fellowship of the church. Inclusive churches often require more interpretation in order for new members to understand what the church believes, what it prizes, how it deals with diversity, and how new members fit into the church. When inclusive churches are slow to incorporate new members, these persons develop patterns of passive participation that are difficult to overcome.

Therefore, it is of great importance that an inclusive church view new member incorporation as an integral part of its discipleship plan. New members need to develop confidence in what they know about a church so that they can more quickly make a contribution. New members need relationships in order to feel accepted, known, and welcomed.

For this reason, we were not drawn to the idea of a new members' class, but rather to a model in which members and prospects (or inactive members who want to get more involved) could experience Christian fellowship while learning information about the church.

After four years of experience with the New Creation Fellowship (NCF), we can see a remarkable difference in the way new members become involved. Often our new members know more about our church than many existing members. They are exposed early, by the pastors and diaconal leaders, to the style of membership that is being sought, but not necessarily realized, within the church. They become leaven in the body, breathing new life and a fresh spirit throughout the existing structures of the church. The intent of NCF is not to isolate new members, but rather to integrate them into the church.

Because First Baptist Church has co-pastors, the NCF meets alternately on the first Friday of each month (September through May) in one of their homes. We meet at 7:30 P.M. for about two hours in an informal atmosphere. We ask prospects and new members to attend six consecutive monthly sessions; however, persons can begin at any session and conclude their commitment six sessions later. We repeat the six-month curriculum cycle as new participants come and go.

We do not require advance notice of attendance. We do state our expectation that new members attend the NCF, but we do not require it. About 75 percent of our new members do participate. Those who do not attend tend not to become active members. One deacon and spouse attend each session, with members of the board sharing the responsibility.

Five major items comprise each session:

A. Relationship-building exercise
B. Basic information about the church
C. Refreshments and informal conversation
D. Opportunities for involvement—current activities and ways to get involved in the church
E. Concluding prayer and devotion.

We will describe items A, B, and D of the model in more detail.

A. Relationship-Building Exercise

The first component of each New Creation Fellowship session is a time to get acquainted, to create *koinonia* (fellowship of believers), and to build trusting relationships. We recognize that the participants often do not know one another, and thus the exercises must not require much personal risk.

Here are the exercises we use in each session.

Session 1: We ask each participant to describe their very first contact with First Baptist Church by asking, "How did you first learn about our church?"

Then, we play a get-acquainted game. We distribute a blank sheet of paper and ask participants to number from 1 to 5 down the left hand side of the sheet. We ask them not to sign their papers. They are asked to complete these statements:

1. My favorite time of year is _____ .
2. The section of the newspaper I read first is _____ .
3. The thing I most wanted to become when I was a child was __ .
4. The one thing I most remember about this past season is ____ .
5. The thing that gives me the greatest satisfaction in life is ____ .

The participants are asked to turn in their papers and are given another blank sheet. The leader reads each list aloud, and participants record the name of the person to whom they think the list belongs. Finally, we go around the circle and ask persons to claim their own statements. This is an enjoyable way to learn more about one another.

Session 2: We use either or both of these exercises, depending upon the size of the group:

SHARING NAMES. We ask participants to tell what they know about their own name: its origin or meaning, any nicknames they might have had, how they feel toward their name, and so on.

SHARING CHURCH HISTORY. We ask participants to share with the group their own personal church history, including what churches they have attended and any particular memories they have about those churches.

Session 3: For this opening exercise, we play a "true or false" game. We ask participants to write down three statements that describe themselves. The statement can be true or false. They have permission to tell a lie if they desire. Then each person reads the three statements while the others mark on a separate sheet whether they believe each statement is true or false. After everyone has shared, we again go around the group and ask each person to admit whether their statements are true or false.

Session 4: In this session we often include a time of sharing about our vocations. We stress that a vocation is not necessarily what you do for money, but the major time investment of your life. We ask such questions as these: What is your vocation? How has it changed over the years? What are its joys or demands? What caused you to choose this vocation? What is a goal you are striving to achieve through your vocation?

Session 5: We use the exercise "My Contribution." We ask participants to complete such statements as:

Something from the past that I have enjoyed doing in a church is

_____ .

The contribution I would most enjoy making to a church is _____

_____ .

A previous highlight in a church for me has been _____

_____ .

Session 6: In this sharing exercise, we focus upon money. We first ask some questions for discussion:

1. How did you first earn money as a child or young person?
2. Do you recall any mistakes you made with money as a child?
3. As an adult, what is your most difficult challenge in relation to how you deal with money?
4. What experiences or models have you had in learning to give money to the church? to those in need?

Then, we distribute the handout about the church budget along with this explanation:

Often the values and priorities of a church can be measured by how its money is used. This exercise helps us explore this area of concern. With a partner, decide how you would like to see the budget amounts on the right matched with the program or budget areas on the left. You do not have to be practical; we do ask that you be faithful to your values.

After completing this, using your best judgement, match up the budgeted amounts with the program areas according to how you actually believe the church budgets its money.

The figures on the worksheet are updated each year, using the latest budget information.

This Year's Church Budget: $306,742.00

Tonight, we consider the program and ministry of First Baptist Church. We begin by recognizing that the values and priorities of a church can in part be measured by how its financial resources are used.

With one partner, decide together how you would like to see the budget amounts on the right (A-I) matched with the program or budget areas on the left (1-9). You don't necessarily have to be practical, just faithful to your own values. Use the "Best of All Worlds" column.

Finally, use the "Realistic" column to place the budget amounts where you think they actually belong.

	Best of All Worlds	Realistic	Budget Amounts
1. Utilities (heat, lights, water)	$_____	$_____	A. $9,050.
2. Worship and Music (music salaries and honoraria, worship supplies, congregational care)	$_____	$_____	B. $81,490.
3. Church Office (secretarial and business-manager salaries, taxes, and benefits; office equipment, supplies, printing, postage, telephone)	$_____	$_____	C. $3,000.
4. Program (theologian in residence, church van, finance campaign, church program, hostess, DABA dues)	$_____	$_____	D. $66,000.
5. Building (custodian salary, maintenance, taxes, assessments, insurance)	$_____	$_____	E. $22,000.
6. Pastoral Ministry (salary, retirement and health insurance, weekday parking fees, auto reimbursement, convention expense, continuing education for pastors, student pastoral associate)	$_____	$_____	F. $52,964.
7. Outreach and Evangelism (advertising, personal witness)	$_____	$_____	G. $26,488.
8. Missions	$_____	$_____	H. $38,540.
9. Christian Education (church school, youth ministry, discipleship education, Missioners)	$_____	$_____	I. $7,210.

B. Basic Information About the Church

We created the curriculum for the six sessions by first asking ourselves, "What does a new member need to know about First Baptist Church in order to become an active, contributing member?" The six sessions are an answer to that question.

Session 1: Our Baptist beliefs and identity
Session 2: First Baptist Church of Dayton, its history and future
Session 3: History of the Baptists in general and American Baptists
            in particular
Session 4: The people of First Baptist Church
            Characteristics of the church's membership and expectations of members
Session 5: Decision-making structure of the church and the role of
            lay leadership
            Distribution of the Church's "Annual Report"
Session 6: The program components of First Baptist Church
            The discipleship plan of the church

We have prepared handouts for each session. We typically lead the participants through the material in the handout, encouraging questions and dialogue along the way. The handouts are more effective if they are brief outlines rather than long narratives. Here is a brief summary of the handouts we distribute:

Session 1 of New Creation Fellowship: "What Do We Believe?"

Our outline highlights our sources of authority, our relations with other churches, our approach to ordinances or sacraments, our response to diversity, our approach to our denomination, and how we interpret the call of the gospel.

Session 2 of New Creation Fellowship: "First Baptist Church—Its History and Future"

We use an outline that highlights the history of our church, leading up to the present day. The final part of the outline shares where the church is today and the apparent direction of its future.

Session 3 of New Creation Fellowship: "Who Are the Baptists?"

We use an outline that highlights the history of the Baptists, how our national denomination is structured, and our church's denominational commitment.

Session 4 of New Creation Fellowship: "First Baptist Church . . . The People, the Members"

We offer a description of our membership by as many categories as possible. We then offer our church's covenant as a statement of what the church expects of its members. We conclude by asking, "What do you expect of your church?"

Session 5 of New Creation Fellowship: "Leadership and Ministry of the Laity"

We offer a worksheet in which we invite discussion regarding the ministry of all Christians and what it means to be "priests to each other." We describe the role of lay leadership within our church, along with an organizational chart of the church.

Session 6 of New Creation Fellowship: "Program Components Within First Baptist Church"

We outline all the programs related to the church year, or those offered by specific groups within the church. We also outline our ecumenical and denominational relationships and agencies with which we cooperate.

D. Opportunities for Involvement

We distribute a sheet entitled "Opportunity Sheet," on which we have listed briefly five to eight activities, events, or volunteer opportunities offered by our church. We do not attempt to make an exhaustive list of ways to become involved, but we do try to offer a variety. Events and activities are described with new persons in mind, unlike most bulletin and newsletter announcements. We briefly highlight this list in the session and offer to answer any questions.

Notes

Chapter 1

[1] Colin Brown, ed., *The New International Dictionary of New Testament Theology*, vol. 1 (Grand Rapids: The Zondervan Corp., 1981), p. 488.

[2] *Ibid.*, p. 490.

[3] Eduard Schweizer, *Lordship and Discipleship* (Naperville, Ill.: Alec R. Allenson, Inc., 1960). pp. 13-14.

[4] Eduard Schweizer, *Jesus*, tr. David E. Green (Atlanta: John Knox Press, 1971), p. 108.

[5] Dietrich Bonhoeffer, *The Cost of Discipleship* (New York: Macmillan, Inc., 1966 ©1959 SCM Press, Ltd.), p. 341.

[6] *Ibid.*, p. 337.

[7] Jon Sobrino, *Christology at the Crossroads: A Latin American Approach*, trans. John Drury (Maryknoll, N.Y.: Orbis Books, 1978), p. 128.

Chapter 2

[1] C. Daniel Batson *et al.*, *Commitment Without Ideology* (New York: The Pilgrim Press, 1973), p. 49.

[2] Dietrich Bonhoeffer, *Christ the Center* (New York: Harper and Row, Publishers, Inc., 1966), p. 61.

[3] Barbara Hargrove and Stephen D. Jones, *Reaching Youth Today: Heirs to the Whirlwind* (Valley Forge: Judson Press, 1983), p. 119.

[4] Urban T. Holmes III, *Ministry and Imagination* (New York: The Seabury Press, Inc., 1976), p. 88.

[5] *Ibid.*

[6] James W. Fowler, in *Hope for the Church: Moltmann in Dialogue with Practical Theology*, ed. Theodore Runyon (Nashville: Abingdon Press, 1979), p. 103.

[7] James E. Loder, *The Transforming Moment: Understanding Convictional Experiences* (San Francisco: Harper and Row, Publishers, Inc., 1981), p. 18.

[8] Fowler, in *Hope for the Church*, p. 101.

[9] *Ibid.*, p. 102.

[10] John B. Cobb, Jr. "Strengthening the Spirit," *Union Seminary Quarterly Review*, vol. 30, nos. 2-4 (Winter-Summer 1975), p. 132.

[11] Fowler, in *Hope for the Church*, p. 109.
[12] J. Sherrell Hendricks *et al.*, *Christian Word Book* (Nashville: Abingdon Press, 1969), p. 108.
[13] Fowler, in *Hope for the Church*, p. 30.

Chapter 3

[1] Floyd V. Filson, *The Layman's Bible Commentary*, Vol. 19 (Atlanta: John Knox Press, 1963), p. 102.
[2] Dietrich Bonhoeffer, *The Cost of Discipleship* (New York: Macmillan, Inc., 1959), p. 99.
[3] Thomas H. Troeger, *Are You Saved? Answers to the Awkward Question* (Philadelphia: The Westminster Press, 1979), p. 96.
[4] *Ibid.*, pp. 92-93.
[5] Dietrich Bonhoeffer, *Christ the Center* (New York: Harper and Row, Publishers, Inc., 1966), p. 61.
[6] Troeger, *Are You Saved?* p. 49.

Chapter 4

[1] Leonard I. Sweet, "Not All Cats Are Gray: Beyond Liberalism's Uncertain Faith," *Christian Century,* vol. 99, no. 22 (June 23-30, 1982), pp. 723-724, copyright 1982 Christian Century Foundation. Used by permission.
[2] Thomas H. Troeger, *Are You Saved? Answers to the Awkward Question* (Philadelphia: The Westminster Press, 1979), pp. 26-27.

Chapter 5

[1] Jon Sobrino, *Christology at the Crossroads: A Latin American Approach,* trans. John Drury, (Maryknoll, N.Y.: Orbis Books, 1978), p. 132.
[2] Theodore Runyon, ed., *Hope for the Church: Moltmann in Dialogue with Practical Theology,* (Nashville: Abingdon Press, 1979), p. 132.